$ix Figure Selling

$$$$

Paul David French

$ix Figure Selling

Copyright © 2016 by Paul David French
All Rights Reserved

No part of this book may be reproduced or transmitted in any form or by any means, graphic, electronic, or mechanical, including photocopying, recording, taping, or by any information storage retrieval system, without written permission of the author.

Printed in the United States of America by
Gorham Printing
Centralia, Washington

Library of Congress
Control Number 2016910699

ISBN 978-0-9850998-2-4

Also by Paul David French
The Awesome Power of No Objection Selling

A Brief Note About This Book

They say *everyone* sells. Professional salespeople, however, depend upon their selling skills for their livelihood.

The ideas in this book represent powerful selling concepts, the application of any one of which will increase your sales effectiveness and your income, as they did mine. Applied together, these ideas allowed me to become the top producing agent in the largest property and casualty insurance company in the State of Michigan during my rookie year, out-selling the hundreds of seasoned sales professionals in my company, and thousands of others in competing companies throughout the state. But the best part is that they allowed me to achieve a solid six figure income in relatively short order.

There are fifty brief chapters within this book. Each chapter contains at least one technique or principle that will help you achieve Six Figure Selling.

As you read, you'll expose your mind to these powerful principles, as well as the anecdotes and examples which demonstrate their practical application.

One of the most important success principles is humor; the ability to enjoy life, to laugh, and to make others laugh.

Combining humor and useful information together results in a more immediate, stronger, and longer lasting effect. In some cases, the humor alone provides a benefit; the anecdote becomes the antidote. This is why every chapter contains something for you to smile about.

So read...and succeed!

4

Contents

	Introduction	7
1	How to Achieve the Irresistible Power of Overwhelming Self Confidence	11
2	How to Be More Welcome Wherever You Go	15
3	How to Optimize Your Compensation Factors to Maximize Your Income	19
4	Buy My Computer!	23
5	Why People Buy	27
6	Lincoln's Key to Success	29
7	Intangible, Invisible, Indispensable!	31
8	The Unbelievable Power of YOUR Subconscious Mind	35
9	Success by Design	37
10	The Source of Inspiration	41
11	How to Expand your Sphere of Influence with a Personal Marketing Plan	43
12	Opportunity Knocks	47
13	Facing the Giants	51
14	The Biggest Mistake Salespeople Make in Selling and How to Avoid It Forever	55
15	Take an Action Toward Your Dreams NOW!	59
16	SUCCESS!	63
17	Objections vs. Conditions	65
18	Finding Customers Vs. Creating Customers	69
19	A True Story	71
20	A Not So True Story	73
21	Getting Your Foot In The Door	75
22	Negotiating Tip Number One: Be Very Clear	79
23	Negotiating Tip Number Two: Avoid Counter Proposals	83

24	Negotiating Tip Number Three: Never Dilute Arguments	85
25	Negotiating Tip Number Four: Avoid Irritators	87
26	Being Proactive in the Selling Business	89
27	Seinfeld on Marketing	93
28	Why Adversity is Your Best Friend	95
29	A Tip for Sales Managers	97
30	The Single Most Important Selling Skill Part I	99
31	The Single Most Important Selling Skill Part II	101
32	To Err is Human	103
33	The Power of the Interrogative?	105
34	The Power of a Positive Mental Attitude	109
35	Seeing Is Believing	113
36	An Outrageous Claim!	115
37	The Awesome Power of a Useful Purpose	117
38	Improved Selling Made Simple	119
39	The Power of Motivation?	123
40	What Are Your Feelings?	125
41	Action This Day	129
42	What's Your Pleasure?	131
43	The Importance of Asking	135
44	A Fantastic Self-Development Resource	139
45	Selling Through the Language Barrier	143
46	Selling in a Facebook World	145
47	Be Prepared	149
48	Smile!	153
49	The Process of Innovation	155
50	How to Achieve an Unfair Competitive Advantage	159
	About the Author	165

Introduction

You hold in your hands a compilation of some of the most powerful concepts, techniques and principles for selling known.

Please don't take the above statement as some kind of ego trip on my part. I'm not taking credit for any of them. I didn't invent them, I didn't reveal them to the world, and I most certainly didn't pioneer their implementation.

I did, however, discover them...for myself, at least. And not a moment too soon!

At the time of my personal revelation, I was selling auto insurance in Detroit, Michigan, and I was failing miserably. I was really down. My self image was so low that if someone were to insult me, I probably would have agreed with them.

In my depressed state, I was so discouraged that I was on the verge of quitting selling altogether. And I would have quit, too, were it not for a man named Jack Hempton.

You see, after seven months in the auto insurance business, I had just experienced my highest single monthly auto insurance sales production–six vehicles insured. Imagine only selling six car policies for the entire month in the automobile capital of the world!

Being an introvert, I hadn't made any friends at work, which only exacerbated my misery. But just as I was preparing to quit and give up on selling forever, Jack Hempton, a fellow sales rep who happened to be working out of the same field office I had been assigned to, reached out to me with a helping hand.

I'll never know why Jack showed an interest in me, but he did, and from that moment forward my life began to change forever. Here's what happened:

Jack took me aside and told me to visit The Church of Today in Warren, Michigan, a suburb of Detroit. This particular church had, at that time, the best book store in the state for purchasing motivational, success oriented, self help materials. It was an amazing treasure trove of books and audio recordings. So I took Jack's advice and purchased three audio cassettes on success and selling.

While I was there, I happened to notice a flyer that announced an all day seminar featuring an Australian businessman by the name of Peter J. Daniels. I didn't know who he was, but the flyer stated that he would shake up my comfort zone. It was scheduled for the following Saturday, so I attended.

At that seminar, Mr. Daniels introduced me to success principles which in very short order changed my life. Within six months of that day, I was the top producing auto insurance agent in the largest auto insurance company in the state of Michigan.

Much of what I learned that day and in the weeks that followed can be found in this book, for within these pages you will find some of the most powerful concepts, techniques and principles on selling known.

This particular book is not unique in this regard, as many books have been published which contain thoughts, ideas, and concepts that have catapulted and transformed the careers and lives of countless people who've read them and then implemented their principles. Examples of such books (and I highly recommend that you read all of them) include:

How to Win Friends and Influence People by Dale Carnegie
The Magic of Thinking Big by Dr. David Schwartz
The Magic of Believing by Claude M. Bristol
The Magic Power of Your Mind by Walter M. Germain
Think and Grow Rich by Napoleon Hill
The Greatest Salesman in the World by Og Mandino
How I Raised Myself From Failure to Success in Selling by Frank Bettger
The Success System That Never Fails by W. Clement Stone
The Power of Positive Thinking by Norman Vincent Peale
How to Reach Your Life Goals by Peter J. Daniels

There is one difference, however, between those great works listed here and this humble tome. While most other books containing success principles require the reader to understand and implement their strategies before positive results can be realized, this book provides one very special benefit for anyone who just reads it, even if they never lift a finger to act on any of the concepts put forward.

In the Bible, the book of Proverbs states, "A merry heart doeth good like a medicine." I believe that the humor you find here will do you some good right away. And as with the life changing principles within this book, I also make no claims of originality on any of the jokes, anecdotes or other light heartedness you'll find within these pages.

I do promise, however, that if you'll take just a few moments as you read each chapter, and highlight or underline any points that you think may be helpful to you, then jot down what you feel is the main theme or principle at the end of the chapter, you'll receive the same benefit from reading this book one time as you would if you were to read it three times without making any such annotations. Then, when you have finished reading this book, go back to the beginning and transfer (or have someone do it for you) the underlined or highlighted phrases and notes onto a separate sheet of paper, or enter it into a word processing document to print out. You'll then have a short list of principles and ideas that you can quickly review on a regular basis. I learned this technique from Peter Daniels, and it has served me well ever since.

Also, forming words or phrases from the first letters of each principle and then committing the resulting acrostic to memory by the use of spaced repetition will allow you to review them anytime, anywhere, and will put them at your command when you need them most...when you are closing a sale!

This is how I used the principles in this book to develop myself into a six figure salesperson. And believe me, if you had known what an analytical, introverted, non-sales type I was during those early years of my sales career, you would know that I speak the absolute truth when I say that if I could do it, you can do it too!

I invite you to contact my office if you have any questions or comments regarding the contents of this book, or if I can be of any assistance to you as you strive to achieve $ix Figure Selling for yourself.

One last point: You'll notice that many of the chapters have a horizontal line dividing them into two sections. This simple device should mark a clear distinction between the joke or fictitious anecdote above and the factual information below.

It should, but don't count on it. ☺

SUCCESS!

Chapter 1

$

How to Achieve the Irresistible Power of Overwhelming Self Confidence

In 1985, a sales manager was in the final stages of hiring a new salesman and was down to the last two candidates, only one of which would get the job.

The first of the final two he interviewed had just graduated from a local community college. "A nice young man," thought the sales manager, "but a bit timid. I want someone who is more confident."

When the first applicant left, the sales manager summoned the second man. "Jim Johansen!" he called. Up stepped a burly man who seemed quite sure of himself.

"This guy looks pretty tough," thought the manager, "he looks like he can handle any situation. I really want to hire him."

"Jim," stated the sales manager, "I like the cut of your jib, and I know a good man when I see one, however, to get this job you must also be intelligent. I see on your application that you forgot to fill in the education section. Where did you receive your formal education?"

"Yale," Jim replied.

"Excellent," declared the sales manager, "I knew that my instincts were correct, they've never failed me yet. You're hired!"

"Now that you're working for us," the manager inquired, "what do you prefer to be called?"

"It doesn't matter," Jim answered, "you can call me Yim or Mr. Yohansen."

Belief in oneself creates a powerful force which can bring about great accomplishments. History has proven this to be true time and again. Early in my selling career, I happened upon a powerful yet amazingly simple technique for developing self confidence to the point of becoming an irresistible force. It's called the Mirror Technique, and I first read about it in a book entitled The Magic of Believing by Claude M. Bristol.

The mirror technique is one method which, although misunderstood and even sometimes made light of, is documented to be psychologically sound and very effective. You can use it to dramatically build your self confidence.

One sales rep who leads his company in sales production swears by it. He says that just before he goes in to meet with a prospect, he will use the rear view mirror in his car to do the mirror technique. He will look into the reflection of his own eyes, and repeat out loud several times a very powerful statement such as "I am an irresistible persuasive force. People are helpless to resist me."

He also states that when he first used this technique he was so persuasive he was shocked. He says that his mind was so much sharper than usual, and he said just the right words to his prospect, things he didn't plan to say. The biggest shock was the way his prospect was so completely impressed, just as he had told himself the prospect would be.

"It's like programming your own outcome to a situation. It's very powerful."

Prove it to yourself. Spend 3 or 4 minutes trying this technique the next time you have to perform at your best.

Start by looking in a mirror, directly into your own eyes, and affirming clearly the outcome that you desire to experience. Always speak in the first person, present tense. Begin with words such as, *I Am, I Have, I Do*, etc.

As you speak the words, try to imagine how experiencing what you are stating will feel. For example, if you are stating, "I am the top sales producer, and I am about to successfully close another sale," try to feel as though you just did what you are stating. Let the emotions and feelings of the success roll over you as you repeat your affirmation to yourself over and over. You are taking control of your thoughts, which dictate your actions, which determine your results.

Next, immediately go into action, and make your sales pitch. It will probably be the best presentation you've ever given, and will lead to the easiest and most profitable sale you've ever made. Over time, you will get better at using this technique, and the results will improve accordingly.

Start today, and very soon you too will possess the irresistible power of overwhelming self confidence!

Chapter 2

$

How to Be More Welcome
Wherever You Go

A traveling salesman was preparing to go back out on the road. He had recently acquired a small puppy, and he was hesitant about leaving the little animal behind, so he sent an email to each of the hotels and motels where he planned to stay during his trip.

He wrote: "I would very much like to bring my little dog with me. He is housebroken and very well behaved. Would you allow me to keep him in my room with me at night?"

As the responses came back, one in particular caught his attention. It read as follows:

I've been operating this hotel for many years and in all that time, I've never had a dog steal towels, sheets, silverware or pictures off the walls. I've never had to evict a dog in the middle of the night for being drunk and disorderly, and I've never had a dog run out on a hotel bill. Yes, your dog is welcome at my hotel, and if your dog will vouch for you, then you are welcome to stay here too."

Michele Monteith is a sales agent for The American Automobile Association, which was for many years the largest property and casualty insurance company in Michigan. AAA had a program called the President's Council, a very exclusive "club" composed of only the top twelve producers in the company, and Michele was a charter member. I learned something from Michele that helped me, and I believe that it can help you too...

In every person's life, there are people who stand out for a very special reason. If you were to list them, it would probably be a very short list. I'm referring to those people who always make you feel welcome! They have a special way about them, so that even if you arrive unannounced, you never feel uninvited.

Michele is such a person. She has a unique way of making people feel special and important. Recently, I dropped in to see her briefly on some business, and in just the few minutes I waited to see her, I overheard several positive comments about Michele from her clients and co-workers.

I've also noticed that whenever her name comes up in conversation, someone always has something nice to say about her. If you ever met her, you'd understand why.

Michele is certainly one of the most positive people I know. She talks in such a way as to make you feel that things are getting better, and she is especially skilled at making you feel good about yourself.

It would be difficult for me to analyze every aspect of just how Michele does this, but two things stand out. Michele smiles a lot, and she shows sincere appreciation. It's no wonder that she is as successful as she is in the world of sales.

Showing appreciation to others without sounding insincere or patronizing requires finesse, because paying a compliment can be a little awkward, especially with people you don't know very well. We may be afraid that they won't accept it graciously and easily because receiving a compliment can sometimes be embarrassing to the recipient.

Early in my selling career I learned a simple technique that instantly solved this problem for me, and it may be of help to you also. It's this: Instead of complimenting the person, compliment the action. Not what a person is, but something a person does. This approach can make all the difference in the world.

For example, make observations about people. If someone seems to have a lot of self confidence, say to them, "You have a lot of self confidence." If someone is very analytical, tell them, "You seem to analyze ideas rather carefully before you accept them." If someone is fun to be with, say, "You're fun to be with."

These brief statements will let people know that you appreciate their qualities without making them uncomfortable. Just make sure that you keep it brief, and never try to explain what you mean. Just state your observation and move on.

Showing sincere appreciation is not always easy, and I have the utmost respect for people who care enough to develop the skills to do it well. I think the world needs more of them.

I'm trying to be more like Michele. I really want to spread some sunshine in people's lives if I can, and I believe emulating Michele can make that possible. It's good for people and it's good for business.

Chapter 3

$

How to Optimize Your Compensation Factors to Maximize Your Income

A federal government employee was sitting in his office and, out of boredom, decided to see what was in his old filing cabinet. He poked through the contents and came across an old brass lamp. There appeared to be some writing on it, and as he rubbed it, a genie suddenly appeared and offered to grant him three wishes.

Stunned and not thinking clearly, the bureaucrat blurted out, "I wish for an ice cold drink right now!"

There was a poof! And out of a puff of smoke a most colorful and delicious looking beverage appeared, complete with ice and a tiny umbrella.

Tasting it, he realized that it was the most delicious drink he had ever experienced. It was cool and refreshing, and drinking it made him feel terrific.

After finishing his drink, he found that he could easily focus his thoughts, and realizing that he was indeed dealing with a powerful genie who could make good on his promise, he stated his second wish.

"I wish to be on a tropical island, surrounded by beautiful women who will do my bidding."

There was another Poof! And when the smoke cleared he felt a cool tropical breeze and realized that he was lounging on a pearl white beach with beautiful women around him, just waiting to please him.

He then told the genie his third and final wish, stating, "I wish to never have to work, ever again."

A final Poof! And when the smoke cleared he found himself alone, back in his government office.

According to the U.S. Bureau of Labor Statistics, there are plenty of six figure income jobs, and not surprisingly, the top ones are in sales. Although it's possible to earn very little in sales if you're new at it, sales is also the highest paying job in America if you know what you are doing.

Looking at those professions where the top 25 percent take home more than $100,000 annually, you'll see that selling is key.

There are dozens of sales positions that often pay in excess of $100,000 per year. It is very common for a top sales producer in virtually every segment of the market to be among the top five percent of earners in the U.S.

Why does selling pay so well?

The answer becomes obvious when you understand the four factors that determine a person's compensation within a free enterprise society.

Firstly, without salespeople, most companies would go out of business, so the demand for an effective salesperson increases their value to the organization. Since the first component of compensation is the *demand for your service*, the more in demand your service is to your employer or whomever is paying you, the more compensation you can command.

Secondly, sales is a tough job to do if you lack the tools and the training, and sadly, most sales organizations fail to adequately provide these two essential components, which is why the churn rate in sales is so high. The tougher it is to find someone who can do the job successfully in spite of these problems, the more valuable that individual is to the organization. The second component of compensation is *replaceability*, or how easy or difficult it is to replace a good salesperson with someone who will perform equally well.

Thirdly, top salespeople close more sales than do average and below average salespeople. They've discovered ways to serve more people in less time. The third component of compensation is the *number of people served.* The more people you serve, the greater will be your compensation.

Finally, since most sales jobs pay based on performance, there is risk involved in taking a job where you could end up earning less than minimum wage. Since *risk* is the fourth factor of compensation, the higher the risk, the higher the reward.

Any one of these factors alone is not indicative of how much money you will make. Serving hundreds of people per day does not necessarily lead to a high income. A fast food employee may serve several hundred people in a single day, but in a low demand way which requires no specialized skills and involves no risk.

Taken together, however, the combination of these components will determine your ultimate compensation because they directly and accurately reflect the value of your service to those who are paying for it.

Find a way to increase one or more of these components and you will have automatically found a way to increase your compensation. It is the opportunity to do this within most sales positions that has made selling the highest paying profession.

22

Chapter 4

$

Buy My Computer!

Salesman: This computer will cut your workload by 50 percent.
Customer: That's great, I'll take two of them.

Traffic was light as I slowly eased my vehicle into the lane. Seventy degrees and sunny, the radio announcer was saying, or something like that. I was a little distracted by the bright sunlight as it reflected intensely off of the chrome of the vehicles in front of me, and even more brilliantly off the windows of several more.

It might have been annoying, except that any day where the sky fades from deep blue overhead to a light blue in the distance without even a hint of a cloud in between, that is a day too perfect for anything as minor as a little glare to bother me. I stopped my vehicle as the traffic signal changed from amber to red.

There were now no vehicles in front of me, as the one just ahead of mine was the last to beat the red light. I patiently waited at the head of the line, satisfied in the knowledge that I was "next." Not that I was really next for anything in particular, but there is something about being at the front of traffic that pleases me. It's like when you're in line at the post office or the bank, and you finally get to the front of the line. You're not being waited on yet, but just that feeling of being "next" is almost a little reward in itself. Funny the little pleasures you enjoy in this life, if you really think about them.

I didn't have time to think about this one for long, however. The traffic light changed, transforming itself from red to green, and as I began to move through the intersection, something caught my eye on the road ahead of me. It was a man crossing the street, but as I approached, I could see the look of recognition on his face. He knew me, but I didn't know him. At least, not at first, but as my vehicle moved closer, I suddenly remembered his face, although I couldn't quite place it. In the few brief moments that elapsed as my vehicle crossed his intended path, I heard three words trail off as I was moving away, and the three words that he shouted at me were, "Buy my computerrrrrrrr!"

Ah ha! Now I remember. He was one of the several salespeople I had spoken with over the last several days while I was shopping for a new computer. I still laugh whenever I remember that moment. The thought of it will probably live with me forever.

I think I saw in that computer salesman an important reason why so many salespeople struggle or wash out altogether. It is the self centered part of us which in truth is the reason we all go off to work every day, and that is, of course, to make our living and provide for ourselves and our families.

Almost everyone who sells for a living does so because they need the money, and while this is not in itself a bad thing, allowing it to drive our selling behavior can be. Even if we're not as obvious as that computer salesman was, we may still be revealing our "need" to make that sale in a subtle way that communicates negative vibes to our prospects, and this can cause us to lose leverage, and possibly cost us sales.

You may be thinking, "Well, sure, but what can I do about it?"

The truth is, the best way to deal with this is to change your paradigm. Completely rethink your reasons for selling. This, in turn, will change the signals that you subconsciously send to your prospects.

For example, I failed miserably in selling until I changed my goal from making sales to helping prospects.

Now, this may sound trite, and if that was all there is to it, it would not have any real power behind it.

I did more, however, than just say I was out to help people. I calculated the dollar value of the savings and benefits that each of my customers were projected to experience as a result of buying from me, and I added this number to a monthly chart. The idea was to serve the public in a specific, tangible way that could be quantified. This chart allowed me to identify, in dollars, the value of the service that I had provided each month.

So I had made getting my commissions the *result* of my labor, and not the *reason* for it, and what a difference this made for me!

I owe this concept to a man by the name of Jack Hempton, who mentored me shortly after I began my sales career.

Why not re-evaluate your reasons for doing what you do. You might just be amazed at the results.

Chapter 5

$

Why People Buy

Three violin manufactures had all done business for years on the same block in the small town of Cremona, Italy.

One day, after years of a peaceful coexistence, the Amati shop hired a new sales manager for $250,000 per year. He decided he had better make his mark right away to increase sales, so he put a sign in the window saying: "We make the best violins in Italy."

The Guarneri shop then hired McKinsey & Company at a cost of $500,000 to advise them. McKinsey sent in a project manager and a crew of consultants, and after exhaustive research and study, they advised Guameri to place a sign in their window proclaiming: "We make the best violins in the whole world," which they did.

Finally, the Stradivarius family spent $5 for a large poster board and a magic marker, and put a sign in the front window of their shop stating: "We make the best violins on the block."

There are many needs in life. Everyone has needs, and because they are needs, most everyone has the same or very similar needs.

If you were to take a look into the checkbooks and credit card statements of 100 people, you would most likely find that they all share many things. Payments to the electric company, phone company, grocery stores and gas stations would all be present. Auto and home insurance, water bill, rent or mortgage payments would also be there.

These needs are commonalities among the most diverse of people. It's safe to say that our needs are what make us the same.

But if this is true, if our needs make us the same, then what makes us different? Would it be fair to suggest that it is our *wants* that define our differences?

Think about it. If you were to examine those same 100 checkbooks and credit card statements, and if the people are from diverse social groups, you would find common needs, but if you separated out the luxuries, or *wants*, I think you'll agree that you'd see very different entries among our 100 subjects.

This leads to the point of selling the want, or desire, rather than the need.

You can convince someone that they need something, but that doesn't mean that they'll buy it, at least not from you.

But if someone *wants* something, they'll find a way to get it, whether they need it or not.

It has been stated that people will forgo their needs, but they'll move heaven and earth to get what they want.

Find out what people want. Appeal to this. Then sit back and watch people gladly hand you their money.

It works every time it's tried.

Chapter 6

$

Lincoln's Key to Success

The following letter was written to one Isham Reavis by Abraham Lincoln while he was living in Springfield, Illinois and before he was elected the sixteenth President of the United States. Lincoln called his letter "Advice to a young boy who aspires to become a lawyer."

In this now famous letter, the future president closes by stating what he believes is the most important attribute to success. I offer this letter from one of the wisest and most respected men in our nation's history as my attempt to convey to you the importance of the power of determination:

> My Dear Sir:
> I have just reached home and found your letter. If you are resolutely determined to make a lawyer of yourself, the thing is more than half done already. It is but a small matter whether you read with anybody or not. I did not read with anyone. Get the books and read and study them till you understand them in their principal features, and that is the main thing. It is of no consequence to be in a large town while you are reading. I read at New Salem, which never had three hundred people living in it. The books, and your capacity for understanding them, are just the same in all places. Always bear in mind that your own resolution to succeed is more important than any other one thing.
> A. Lincoln

Chapter 7

$

Intangible, Invisible, Indispensable!

Question: How many salespeople does it take to change a light bulb?

Answer: None. The top producer threatens to go work for the competition if something isn't done about the terrible lighting situation, and the rest of the salespeople say that there's no commission for changing light bulbs. Then the sales manager, who's always complaining that "In order to get something done right I have to do it myself," takes the initiative and proceeds to screw the light bulb into the water faucet.

Have you noticed that pretty much every sales organization seems to have one or two people who produce many times more than the average?

Why is this, do you think?

I could probably cite dozens of different reasons, but you know, we can get so confused by the complexity of something that sometimes what we really need is a blinding flash of the obvious.

I once read that after the civil war was over they asked General Pickett what lead to the failure of "Pickett's Charge." He replied that he always thought the Yankees had something to do with it.

So, if we reexamine our question in this light, why do some salespeople produce so much more than the rest, do you suppose it's possible that they might *know* something that the others don't?

This may sound like an obvious explanation, but often the greatest secrets are hidden in plain sight. For example:

Did you know that if you were to weigh one of NASA's space craft before launch on a very sensitive and accurate scale, you would know the exact weight of the *entire* device, including its payload, booster engines, main engines, fuel, guidance system, sensors...the entire system.

And if you were to then remove any one of its components, right down to the smallest screw, the weight would be affected, and you would know that something has been removed just by measuring the difference in the weight. This data would tell you that the mechanism has been altered in some way.

But there is one component of the space craft that, if completely removed, would totally disable the devise, yet the removal could *not* be detected by weighing it. Can you guess to which component I'm referring?

I'm not talking about disconnecting wires or damaging parts, but rather the *total removal* of an essential component from the whole.

The component that can be completely removed without affecting the mass or weight of the space craft in any way is, of course, the guidance program–the information telling the computers how to control the vehicle in flight.

You see, information is the one component that has no mass or physical form, yet without information, everything else is worthless at best, and harmful at worst.

It's impossible to see the information inside the heads of top salespeople. The only way of knowing what's in there is to observe what they say and do, and that's probably a good start to becoming a top performer.

They say that the best experience is other people's experience. It's always less costly and less painful to learn from someone else's mistakes, isn't it?

I'm amazed by how many sales organizations have top producers who out perform the rest, yet are not tapped to help develop the other salespeople in the proper way. For example, one very large organization demanded that their sales people set between 12 and 15 appointments per week. To get in front of that many people required meeting with anyone who would agree to an appointment, regardless of how unqualified a prospect they may have been. This involved using a very aggressive approach to appointment setting, and not taking "no" for an answer.

The top producer of the organization, however, only set four to six appointments per week, and he consistently out performed nearly everyone else in that organization.

This top achiever knew something that the other sales reps and even the management of the organization didn't understand. He realized that sales are not made by wasting time with non-buyers. He also knew that success in sales doesn't come from trying to persuade non-buyers to buy, but rather, it comes from knowing when to take "no" for an answer. Sorting, rather than persuading, was this sales rep's key to consistently and easily earning a six figure income.

Ultimately, the difference between his and everyone else's sales results was what he knew about sorting–taking "no" for an answer–and moving on. It was this knowledge in his head that is intangible and invisible, yet completely indispensable.

And now you know what he knows.

Chapter 8

$

The Unbelievable Power of YOUR Subconscious Mind

A man and his wife were driving through the beautiful Welsh countryside one day when they came across a road sign which read:

"Llanfairpwllgwyngyllgogerychwyrndrobwllllantysilio gogogoch" (The longest town name in the United Kingdom).

The husband pronounced the name and his wife laughed. "That's not how you pronounce it," she said, and proceeded to pronounce it herself. Her husband nearly crashed the car laughing, and they started debating about how to properly pronounce the name of the town.

Well the debate soon became heated and as it was approaching lunch time they decided to pull into a restaurant in the town whose name was the subject of their argument. As they were paying their bill, the wife asked the cashier, "Excuse me, but would you mind settling an argument between my husband and me? Could you possibly pronounce the name of where we are, only please do it very slowly."

So the cashier leaned forward and in her thick Welsh accent said, "Buuuuurrrrrr-gggggerrrrrrrrrrr Kiiinggggg."

Please look carefully at the following paragraph. At first glance, it may appear unintelligible, but you'll soon find that reading it is much easier than you would have first believed.

Eevn thuogh almsot ervey wrod is cpeomlltey scrmeabld, the phaonmneal pweor of yuor mind is enbanlig you to raed it! Eevn yuor cpuotemr's splel cehck cnanot dhsieper tehse wdors, but you can! As lnog as the fsirt and lsat ltteers are in the ceorrct ptisoion, tehn the oredr of the rset of the ltteers deons't mttaer. A rscheearch taem at Cmabrigde Uinervtisy has daetmoenstrd taht your biran deos not raed ervey lteter iildlviduany, but rethar it preocesss the wrod as a wlohe. If you can do this wthiuot raelly eevn tnyrig, waht oethr tignhs can you aiompcclsh if you put yuor mnid to it? This is a tesmitnet to the phaonmneal pweor of yuor sbucnosiocus mind!

Chapter 9

$

Success by Design

Reaching the end of a job interview for an entry level insurance sales position, the sales manager asked the applicant, "And what starting salary were you looking for?"

The candidate replied, "In the neighborhood of $100,000 a year, depending on the commission structure and benefits package."

The sales manager said, "Well, what would you say to a $110,000 salary *plus* 110 percent first year commission *plus* a quarterly bonus *plus* five weeks paid vacation *plus* full medical and dental *plus* a company matching retirement fund *plus* a company car *plus* a generous expense account?"

The applicant perked right up and blurted out, "You're kidding!"

To which the sales manager responded, "Yes, I am...but you started it."

Imagine creating an above average income in the selling profession, one that would be the envy of most sales professionals...and then doubling it! How about quadrupling it? Can the thoughts and ideas of someone who has done this benefit you?

For some sales professionals, being successful and developing a leadership position within their industry is the pinnacle of a rewarding career, but for others, it's just the beginning. Charles D. Epstein, CLU, ChFC, of Epstein Financial Services, Springfield, Mass, is one such individual. He is a financial advisor who achieved success in selling early on, qualifying for the Million Dollar

Round Table in 1980, his first year in the business. He has continued to out perform the average, consistently turning in top production numbers, having achieved Top of the Table status.

But he didn't stop there. Driven to excel even further, and possessing a deep commitment to the success of family owned businesses throughout New England, Charles used his success as a foundation for even greater achievements. In 1992 he founded the UMASS Family Business Center at the University of Massachusetts. Charles is now the Advisory Chair at the Center and one of the first Certified Family Business Specialists in America by the American College.

Oh, and one other thing. Charles says positioning himself within his community as a trusted advisor and expert has allowed him to quadruple his already substantial income in only five years!

I asked Charles to share with me some of his ideas for achieving top performance in selling. He was quick to point out that change is a major factor which must be addressed. For him, integrating change into his planning is natural because, as he puts it, "This business has changed every six months since I've been in business...all I know is change."

With this in mind, Charles then suggests that you differentiate yourself in a creative fashion. For example, one year his company hosted 450 of his top customers at a local theater, where they were be treated to music, hors d'oeuvres and a performance of *A Chorus Line*. This is one way of keeping in touch and standing out at the same time.

Another way Charles steps it up is that he takes his clients out to breakfast or lunch on their birthday with no obligation to talk business! And of course, Charles doesn't overlook the usual methods of keeping in touch as all of his clients receive a birthday card each year.

Charles is very committed to the success of his clients. Every quarter, his firm sends out more than 2,000 newsletters providing them with valuable information on topics such as estate planning, family budgeting, and taxes, just to name a few.

How does he find the time to do so much? Charles advises that, as soon as you can afford to, you should delegate as many of these tasks and activities as possible. In fact, he recommends having a staff member whose sole job is to be a customer contact expert. This way you can provide the highest level of contact without sacrificing those activities that got you your customers in the first place.

Try implementing some of Mr. Epstein's ideas today. His success is a testimony to the effectiveness of keeping in touch and doing those things which result in six figure selling.

Chapter 10

$

The Source of Inspiration

Dan was like any father; he was very concerned about the proper care and feeding of his baby. In other words, he left those tasks to the baby's mother, his wife, Dorothy.

But in 1927, Dorothy realized that it made no sense for her to be struggling with the tedious and messy process of mashing and straining vegetables to feed her baby when her husband could be doing it for her…in his canning plant located in Fremont, Michigan. She encouraged him to puree the food and put it in cans, and that's how Dan and Dorothy Gerber started what would become the Gerber baby food company.

The source of inspiration is most often the answer to a question. You pose this question to yourself, sometimes purposefully and out loud, but more often silently, subtly, maybe even subconsciously. You ask yourself, "Is there a better way?" Your mind then Googles itself for the answer, and that answer may come to you instantly, or it may come later, while your thoughts are on something else entirely, and in a flash–Eureka!–and you have your idea.

Consider the following:

Ole Evinrude couldn't row his boat across the lake fast enough lake to keep his girlfriend's ice cream from melting. He asked himself, "Is there a better way?" Result: the outboard motor.

A housekeeper kept breaking her employer's fine china when she washed it by hand. Her employer wondered, "Is there a better way?" Result: the automatic dishwasher.

Edward Land's daughter didn't want to have to wait to see the pictures she took with her camera. She asked her father, "Is there a better way?" Result: the Polaroid instant camera.

A German immigrant's customers were taking home the silk gloves he provided to serve bratwurst in his restaurant. He asked himself, "Kann es irgendwie besser gemacht werden?" and the answer came when it occurred to him to split a bun and place the bratwurst inside. Result: the hot dog.

Conclusion: Put your mind to work for you. Ask yourself, "Is there a better way?" Then be patient. In due time, your answer will come, and when it does, you will know that you have discovered the secret of how to tap into the source of inspiration.

Chapter 11

$

How to Expand your Sphere of Influence with a Personal Marketing Plan

Bob was so excited about his promotion to Vice President of Sales that he kept bragging about it to his wife for weeks on end.

Finally, she could take it no longer, and told him, "Listen, Bob, that title doesn't mean anything anymore. VPs are a dime a dozen. They even have a VP of Corn down at the grocery store."

"Really?" he said. Unsure of whether this was true or not, Bob decided to call the grocery store.

A clerk answered and Bob asked, "Can I please speak with the Vice President of Corn?"

To which the clerk replied, "Canned or frozen?"

Would you like to maximize your success and take your career to the next level?

One sales professional who recently made the decision to do just that is Mike, a reasonably successful sales rep for a large financial services firm in the Midwest. Mike has been selling for 20 years, and has a sizable clientele. Over the years, he has developed and implemented plans for prospecting, appointment setting, presenting, and closing. He has read several books on sales and has taken numerous classes and seminars. In spite of this, his job has become rather mundane, and the excitement that he felt early in his career has faded. Mike wants to make his job, and his life, more interesting and rewarding.

The fact is, many sales professionals can relate to Mike. Are you one of them? Would you like to make your job more interesting, and spice up your life vis-à-vis your

43

career? If your answer is "yes," then perhaps a Personal Marketing Plan may be the answer for you.

Question: Do you have a personal marketing plan, one that helps you to successfully market yourself to your world?

Successful sales professionals understand the importance of a *professional* marketing plan as a systematic way to expand and maintain their customer base. In this way, they are able to effectively market their product or service, and experience the results necessary to be successful in the selling business. Designing and implementing a *personal* marketing plan can result in much greater personal success, and even help move you to the next level in your career.

But how, you may be asking, can a personal marketing plan help me? There may be several ways that you can benefit. Consider the following:

1) If you are currently involved in personal sales, marketing yourself will most certainly enhance your efforts in promoting your product or service, which will result in an immediate sales production increase.

2) Marketing yourself will also help you become more in tune with your own talents, abilities, and strengths relative to both your current position and other opportunities which may exist for you now.

3) Marketing yourself will help you identify possibilities for your future which you might never have considered if your marketing efforts involved only your product or service.

Still not sure if a personal marketing plan is right for you? Consider Fred Grandy. As an actor, he is best remembered as "Gopher" Smith from the TV series *The Love Boat*. Congressman Grandy successfully leveraged his notoriety to win two consecutive terms in the US House of Representatives. He once stated that he learned early on in his first campaign that while he still had to bring his message to the people, probably 80 percent of the game was simply getting his name known. He acknowledged that *The Love Boat* did that for him, giving him a tremendous advantage as an emerging political candidate.

Having a major network series promote you to millions of television viewers week after week may not be in your future, but the concept of personal marketing can still work for you on whatever level you're currently operating, so if you wish to develop a plan of your own, here are a few thoughts to consider:

Mapping out your tactics is a good beginning for any personal marketing plan, especially since no plan is of any value if it does not consider the strengths and weaknesses of the individual or individuals who must carry it out. So begin by determining exactly what you can and cannot do, and just as important, what you are and are not willing to do to become known and recognized by your public.

Having done this, however, it is important to consider the long term effects of your plan, in concert with your long term goals, and develop a strategy for implementing it. Some questions to ask yourself in doing this might include: What do I really want to be doing with my time in service to others between now and when I retire? How great an impact do I wish to have on my community? What type of people will I need to help me accomplish this? How can I attract these people to me so that I can learn from them?

One key factor in advancing your career is to insure that you meet or exceed your individual goals by specifically maximizing your results every step of the way. Turning every goal into a major campaign creates urgency, excitement, and guarantees a better result.

For example, Jack, an experienced sales rep, had recently changed employers. Jack had made up his mind that he was going to sell 80 units for the month, a feat that had never been accomplished at his new company. He made it clear to everyone involved that he was willing to do whatever it takes to succeed. Late into the month and having nearly achieved his goal, Jack was observed pacing the floor of the office, repeating over and over to himself, "I need 10 more, I need 10 more…" Jack did meet his goal, and you can bet that his success came with a great feeling of power and elation.

Another idea you should never overlook is tapping the minds and talents of others who have the success that you desire. The principle of association is a powerful force that can help you tremendously. Determine to market yourself to those people who are already where you wish to be. This concept was understood well by David Ogilvy, the great advertising guru. When he started his firm, he made a list of all of the major accounts he wanted to acquire, big accounts that most new people in the business would never dream of getting. It took time, but eventually, he got them all.

The truly driven professional never overlooks the opportunity to seek help from those who best know the ropes, even if he has to pay for the privilege. The old saying, "A jack of all trades is a master of none," still has relevance. Don't try to be an expert at everything. By remaining focused on those things that you know, you will accelerate your advancement toward your ultimate goals. Those areas where you have little or no knowledge can be a dangerous distraction to you if you expend your time, talent, and other resources on them. You can accomplish much more in less time by paying a professional to help than you might accomplish in many days or weeks of expending your own efforts, given your lack of expertise and the learning curve involved.

Don't wait! Outline a personal marketing plan and then get busy filling in the details, then put it into action.

Chapter 12

$

Opportunity Knocks

A retired couple moved to California and purchased a home overlooking the ocean. They would often sit on their balcony and watch the activity on the public beach below.

They began to notice that almost every day, one particular girl would approach people who were sitting on the beach, glance around, then speak to them.

Usually, the people would shake their head "no" or wave her off and she would move along, but occasionally someone would nod and there would be a quick exchange of money for something she carried in her bag. The couple assumed that she was selling drugs, but since they didn't know for sure they just continued to watch, and did nothing.

After a couple of weeks, however, the wife noted to her husband, "Honey, I noticed that she usually only approaches people with radios and other electronic devices. Tomorrow, why don't you get a towel and our big radio and go lie out on the beach and see what she does."

The plan worked perfectly, and the wife was busting with anticipation when she saw the girl talking to her husband. As he walked back up from the beach, she excitedly went out to met him. "Well, is she selling drugs?" she inquired.

"No, she isn't." he said, "she's selling batteries."

"Batteries?" cried the wife.

"Yes," he replied. "She sells C cells by the seashore!"

It was a beautiful Michigan summer day in July of 1970 as a brand new Chevy convertible traveled west along Eight Mile Road in East Detroit (since renamed Eastpointe). As the driver stopped for a traffic light, the sounds of Ernie Harwell announcing the play-by-play along with the roar of the fans filling the old stadium at the corner of Michigan and Trumbull could be heard coming from the radios of several vehicles waiting at the intersection. The brilliance of the sparkling paint and the shine of the abundant chrome bumpers and other appointments of this top of the line model attracted admiring looks from drivers and pedestrians alike, giving the owner of this Chevy the famous "pride of ownership" feeling that automobile companies strive so hard to achieve.

As the light changed to green, the driver turned right and headed north on Gratiot Avenue for a short distance, then, turning right onto the lot of Gene Merollis Chevrolet, he headed toward the building labeled "New Car Sales." Pulling his vehicle into a parking space, the driver is met by Joe, the salesman who sold him the vehicle just a few weeks before.

Having received a call only an hour earlier letting him know that his customer would be coming by with a problem, Joe now looks genuinely concerned and gets right down to business. He asks the vehicle's new owner to please explain the exact nature of the problem he is experiencing. The owner raises the hood and directs Joe to listen closely to the engine.

"There's a strange knocking sound, Joe, I don't think it's supposed to sound like this. What do you think?"

Joe knows that the knocking sound he's hearing is not normal, and will require the attention of a staff mechanic, but to Joe, this is literally the sound of *opportunity knocking*.

Joe Girard is listed in the Guinness Book of Records as the world's greatest salesman. For 12 straight years Joe sold more cars and trucks than any other salesperson in the business, selling more than twice as many vehicles as the nation's number two producer. In fact, during his fifteen year selling career, Joe sold 13,001 cars and trucks–more than most car *dealerships* sold in the same period! And every one of them was an individual, face to face sale–Joe was not involved in fleet sales.

While Joe is famous for the outstanding work and signature techniques he used to *get* his record breaking sales numbers, Joe became known among his thousands of customers for what he did for them *after the sale*. In fact, in the bestselling book, *In Search of Excellence* by Tom Peters and Robert Waterman, Joe is quoted as stating to his customers, "I want to sell you a lemon."

Clearly, Joe did not want his customers to be unhappy with their purchase. What he meant by his controversial statement is that his greatest opportunity to distinguish himself among other salespeople *to his customers* comes when they have a problem. It is at that time that Joe is able to demonstrate to his people in a tangible fashion the reason why they made the right decision by buying from him. His ability to make his customer's problems his problems allowed Joe to get more referrals and repeat business than any other sales rep in the largest selling car company in America. Joe's success in getting the various other departments of the dealership to perform to resolve problems and fully satisfy the customer, all the while giving the customer complete confidence that everything will be fixed so as to reduce or eliminate the stress they were experiencing, is the real reason Joe was able to accomplish so much more than any of his peers in the new car sales business.

What is the point of all of this? Simply to say that customer problems are your greatest opportunities for referrals and repeat business, because only when a customer experiences a problem do you have the chance to really go above and beyond what they are expecting from a salesperson. If you solve a customer's problem with courtesy, skill, and enthusiasm, you will pretty much win that customer over for life.

Chapter 13

$

Facing the Giants

Bob stood at the bedside of his fabulously wealthy yet gravely ill father. The doctor had stated that it was only a matter of days until Bob's dad would be gone, at which time Bob would inherit his father's entire fortune of over twenty million dollars.

Bob decided that he needed a woman to enjoy it with, so he went to a singles bar where he spotted the most beautiful woman he had ever seen. Her natural beauty took his breath away.

After several failed attempts to arouse her interest, he finally decided to use his secret weapon by informing her of his financial situation. This impressed her greatly, and her attitude towards him changed immediately. She even agreed to go home with him that evening.

Bob did not understand that women think differently than men.

Three days later, she became Bob's stepmother.

You've heard of David vs. Goliath, haven't you? How a small shepherd boy went up against the biggest warrior in the land with only a sling and a few stones, and defeated him on the field of battle?

Well, imagine David's little sister going up against an ARMY of Goliaths with no sling and no stones. Then read on to discover Jennifer Gallardo's story ...

Jennifer started her business in the Portland, Oregon area in 1998. At that time, she was going up against well entrenched competition that was literally spending tens of millions of dollars on advertising in her local market to keep small, non-traditional competitors such as herself from getting a foothold. Jennifer intuitively knew that she needed to implement guerrilla marketing, and what she did next will inspire you.

You see, Jennifer is a midwife, and her competition is only the multi-billion dollar western healthcare industry. And with virtually unlimited resources and an established position in the minds of…well…everybody, the traditional healthcare business in general and the Obstetrics and Gynecology fields in particular had about a million to one advantage over Jennifer from day one.

So here's how Jennifer began what would become the most successful business in its field in the Pacific Northwest: Andaluz Waterbirth Centers.

Jennifer started by calling people…lots of people. She looked for every opportunity she could find to get herself in front of pregnant women; speaking in classroom settings, setting up parties, and networking as though her life depended on it.

She introduced herself to every pregnant woman she saw…anywhere…and made sure that she gave them her business card *and* got their name and phone number so that she could contact them to set an appointment. Then when she called them, she let them know that the first appointment would be free so they would be motivated to see what this "waterbirth" thing was all about.

During that first appointment, or "interview" as she calls it, Jennifer would ask the mothers-to-be very specific questions about the kind of "vision" they had for their baby's birth. Jennifer would have them expand on that vision, and soon they could start to see waterbirth as a part it. Then Jennifer made sure to always transition the first interview directly into a free prenatal care session so as to immediately allow the "prospect" to know what it would feel like to be a "customer."

Jennifer worked hard, but she also worked smart. She asked herself, "What can I do that the big hospitals and other traditional medical establishments can't or won't do?" Jennifer got her answer, and she used the smallness of her business to her advantage by providing personal care…really, really personal care. She and her staff have since established a reputation for caring like no other I've seen in this or any other industry.

I want to close this chapter by offering just a few excerpts from comments given by actual customers of Andaluz Waterbirth Centers. Ask yourself what you would do to receive endorsements like these from YOUR customers:

"Thank you! Thank you! A million thank yous! Thank you all so much for your expertise and professionalism, but most of all for your wonderful warm hearts…"

"Thanks for your INCREDIBLE patience and support. I couldn't have come through it a success without your help. We will definitely be back…I will continue to recommend the center to all I know."

"The compassion, knowledge and support we were given by your staff has left a lasting mark on our lives…"

"I just want to thank you, though these words seem so trivial compared to what I feel…I pray rich blessings on what you do…"

"Thank you for your warmth and love, it made us feel at home…"

"Thank you all for the tender loving care we received…our experience here was far better than we dreamed. We held high expectations and you surpassed them all!"

"What a wonderful blessing you were to us."

Chapter 14

$

The Biggest Mistake Salespeople Make in Selling and How to Avoid It Forever

Rule #1 - If you don't give your customer what he wants, someone else will.

Rule #2 - See Rule #1.

There is one selling principle, which if placed at the forefront of your thinking, and made to be your number one priority in your sales approach, will increase your selling effectiveness automatically. Sales reps who've learned and implemented this principle have seen their results increase immediately and dramatically.

You won't have to learn new closing techniques, work longer hours or work harder. You won't even need to make additional sales calls. You will, however, reap huge rewards as if you had done those things.

For example, after learning about this rule, one sales rep closed more sales in the following month than he had closed in the previous four months combined!

Other reps have gone from average (or in many cases below average) performers to top producers almost overnight.

Even seasoned veterans have experienced an "awakening" when exposed to this concept for the first time, and have gone on to sell more of their products and services faster and easier. Would you like to experience similar results?

If your answer is "yes," then I believe you'll be closing more sales soon, because you have just experienced the effect of careful application of the principle.

Have you guessed what it is yet?

Here's a hint: After having just read the preceding information about this principle, how do you now feel about it?

Is it safe to say that you *want* to learn more?

Because the principle I'm referring to is simply this: People will forgo their needs, but *they will move heaven and earth to get what they want.*

Yes, it's very simple, but you must apply this rule in every aspect of your sales approach.

Are you trying to "sell the need" and missing sales that you really believe you should be getting? Are you trying to use "benefits selling" to get people to buy? Are you trying to apply "consultative selling" to make the sale?

None of the above methods work on every qualified prospect, because every qualified prospect doesn't always *want* the same thing, yet when these various approaches *do* work, we become fooled into thinking that it was the method that was successful.

The reality is, the prospect doesn't buy because of a specific method or technique, but rather they buy because they want what you're selling *more* than they want what it costs to buy it, that being time, effort, money, security, or risk.

Or they buy because they want what you're selling more than the consequences of not having it.

Regardless of which reason applies, *both* of them begin with the same five words: They buy because they *want*.

Do this: Realize that people only buy what they want. Then find the best way to communicate to them that buying what you're selling will give it to them.

What to say, and how to say it, and what to do, and how to do it, will become apparent to you if you just keep telling yourself, "People will forgo their needs, but they'll move heaven and earth to get what they want."

When you do this, the close will not be a tug of war, or an exercise in cleverness on your part. The close will instead simply become the logical conclusion to an effective and timely sales presentation, because they'll want what you're selling, and they'll know it.

I can honestly say that I've never made a "difficult" sale since I began applying this principle over 30 years ago. In fact, virtually every time I set an appointment to meet with someone about buying my product or service, I made a sale. And they bought easily. Sometimes I didn't even have to ask for the order, they just gave it to me.

Find people who *want* what you have, and they *will* buy.

And in the process of seeking out people who want your product or service, you'll undoubtedly come across qualified prospects who don't want it *yet*. If this is the case, plant a seed, and move on. Respect their decision, give them the soaking time they want, and you'll gain their trust.

Now, go out there and find people who want what you have, then, help them get it!

Chapter 15

$

Take an Action Toward
Your Dreams NOW!

Two boys were playing football in Central Park when one of them was suddenly attacked by a pit bull. Thinking quickly, the other boy ripped off a board from a nearby fence, wedged it down the dog's collar and twisted it, breaking the dogs neck.

A sports reporter who was strolling by saw the incident and rushed over to interview the boy.

"Young Giants Fan Saves Friend From Vicious Animal," he began writing in his notebook.

"But I'm not a Giants fan," the little hero replied.

"Sorry, since we're in New York, I just assumed that you were." said the reporter, and he began writing again. "Little Jets Fan Rescues Friend From Horrific Attack."

"I'm not a Jets fan either," the boy said.

"I assumed everyone in New York was either for the Giants or the Jets. What team do you root for?" the reporter asked.

"I'm a Cowboys fan," the child said.

In that evening's newspaper, the headline in the sports section read, "Little Redneck Maniac Kills Beloved Family Pet."

I'm not much of a sports fan anymore.

It may be okay for some people, but for me, getting all caught up in a game was great when my team was winning, but when they lost, I felt like I had personally lost as well. It drained me as though I was the one on the field getting beaten up.

So one day I just decided that I wasn't going to invest any more of my emotional energy into anything for which I could not personally control the outcome.

I still get a kick out of those middle aged overweight men who show up at sporting events wearing body paint and holding those big signs that say "We're number one." Are they number one? No, the athletes on the team may be number one in their division, or even the league, but these fans are just a bunch of out of shape couch potatoes trying to feel successful as a result of someone else's accomplishments.

Hey, I'm not against sports, I'm just against getting emotionally involved if I can't personally control, or at least have some impact, on the outcome.

Think I'm being a bit hard on these guys? Maybe so, but such is the way of the masses, people who live for the weekend, people who lead lives of quiet desperation.

Are you one of these people? Or do you have higher aspirations than to live vicariously through a team of people who will never even know your name? I hope that you have more going on in your life than that. I hope that your work allows you to accomplish something that lets you express yourself and brings more meaning to your life than just a paycheck and a place to go between weekends.

But if you find yourself stuck in the "rut" where so many people are content to exist, at least recognize it, and *do something to change your life*!

Take an action today! Write up a new plan. Make a call, write a letter, or talk to someone who already has what you want and ask them to help you get yours. Do something, anything to get you back on the track that got you so excited back when you *were* excited about life. You *remember* those days, don't you?

I apologize if this does not apply to you. If you're progressing toward a worthy goal and feel that this chapter is off the mark for you, that's great! Good for you, and I'm very, very glad.

On the other hand, if these words have hit the mark for you, there is good news. You can change your life by changing your attitude, and your attitude can start to change by taking an action in the right direction.

W. Clement Stone always said that emotions are not always subject to the will, but they are always subject to *action*.

So take action. Any action. As long as it will bring you a little bit closer to your dream, whatever it may be. You'd be surprised how fast a couple of baby steps can begin to build momentum.

Somewhere out there among the readers of this book are people who need a pat on the back or a shot in the arm. If you're one of them, take heart. I believe in you!

Now go ahead and take action!

Chapter 16

$

SUCCESS!

Can you explain the meaning of the word *success*?

Success has been defined in many ways by many people. Some have stated that success is the progressive realization of a worthy ideal. Others have said that success is the willingness to bear pain. Still others believe that success is simply the opposite of failure.

The opposite of failure. That sounds about right, doesn't it?

Or does it?

George Burns must have known a lot about success. He lived to be 100, and he lived pretty well. Here's what he thought about it:

"I honestly think it is better to be a failure at something you love than to be a success at something you hate."

Since it is reasonable to conclude that the "better" thing would make you more *personally* successful, it seems that what Mr. Burns was really saying is that we may at times become more of a success by failing than by succeeding.

Possibly the most important man of the 20th century, Sir Winston Churchill, had his own idea of success. Notice what he had to say about it:

"Success is going from failure to failure without a loss of enthusiasm."

So here we have another fantastically successful person who also likens success to failure. Can it be that failure is not the opposite of success after all?

Let's ask Malcolm Forbes. Although no longer with us, Mr. Forbes was no stranger to success, and the Magazine that bears his name continues to chronicle the achievements of the wealthiest people in the world. He expressed his idea of success and failure this way:

"Failure is success if we learn from it."

So it would appear that failure is proving to be an important component of success.

Some of the most successful people throughout history have stated that failure is the foundation of success. Or put another way, General George S. Patton said:

"Success is how high you bounce when you hit bottom."

I hope that you are never discouraged by your so called "failures," and that you always bounce back higher than you had ever imagined you could. My wish for you, as always, is simply…

SUCCESS!

Chapter 17

$

Objections vs. Conditions

A new salesman was calling on one of the prospects on his lead list, the Director of a mental asylum.

Remembering his sales training, and desiring to make a good impression before he began his sales presentation, the salesman decided to get the Director talking about himself by asking him some questions about his work. He began by asking the Director what the criterion was for determining whether or not a patient should be institutionalized.

"Well," said the Director, "we fill up a bathtub, then we offer the patient a teaspoon, a teacup and a bucket and ask him or her to empty the bathtub."

"Oh, I understand," said the salesman, "a normal person would use the bucket because it's bigger than the spoon or the teacup."

"No." said the Director, "A normal person would pull the plug. Do you want a bed near the window?"

How do you sell without ever overcoming objections?

To properly explain this within the confines of a single chapter, it is necessary to fast forward to the close. I define the close as the logical conclusion to an effective and timely sales presentation.

It's at this point in the sales process that people have to decide whether to take action and buy–or not. People *will* buy if they want what you're selling more than they want what it costs to buy it (time, money, effort, risk, reputation). Or, they'll buy if they want what you're selling more than they want to deal with the consequences

65

of *not* buying. In other words, people will buy if they *want* what you're selling.

Regardless of whether they intend to buy or not, at this point prospects may put up some resistance. Salespeople refer to this resistance as *objections*, and immediately go into the "overcoming objection" mode. However, by definition, an objection is when the prospect objects to something the salesperson did or said. In other words, the salesperson is being objectionable by trying to get the prospect to buy something that they are not yet mentally prepared to buy.

We find that your prospects may just be setting *conditions* which have to be met before they can or will buy. This may involve helping them to justify the price. Or, it may require them to read some literature or study some cost data. Many people are afraid of buying something, even if they want to buy it, without first justifying their purchase with some study or reflection, or both.

Often, they may conceal their real concern by stating things like, "I need to think about it" or "I need to study this before I make a decision." Many people are just afraid of taking action before they've done their due diligence. Whatever it is, they'll tell you what they really want if you'll just let your guard down and listen carefully.

When they state their "objection," ask questions such as, "Is that your only reason" and "in addition to that, would there be any other reason for not going ahead with this?" Keep pumping them for any additional reasons why they won't buy until you get to the *real* reason. It's pretty common that the last reason they provide is the real one.

When they run out of reasons, discuss these conditions and nail down exactly what they require to meet them. Resist the temptation to try to "overcome their objections." Don't do it, because a condition is not an objection, and treating it as a condition allows you to

66

clarify and better communicate to them that you understand their problems.

Next, use the "just supposing" technique to be sure that you haven't overlooked an important condition. Ask them questions like: "Just supposing that we were able to meet the conditions that you outlined, would you then want to go ahead and place your order?" If they say yes, ask them why. Try to get to the heart of the issue. Focus on why they want it rather than why they don't. Then arrange to fulfill their conditions and close the deal. If they say no, then they don't want what you are selling, at least not now. Move on to your next prospect. Don't waste time with non-buyers.

Now, I realize that my last point goes completely against the grain of traditional selling. We've all heard things like, "The sale doesn't start until you get your first no," or, "Always be closing," or, "Don't quit until you get ten of no's."

I've even consulted with very large, well known companies in the USA that instruct their people not to give up until the prospect either buys or hangs up on them! I refer to this behavior as "leaving a trail of bodies in your wake" and it is completely unacceptable. Unfortunately, it's also more common than you might think.

The good news is, there *is* a better way! In most cases, buyers will buy with absolutely no objections at all if you simply appeal to what they want and make provision for their conditions in advance of the close. The close, after all, is supposed to be the logical *conclusion* to an effective and timely sales presentation.

Salespeople who have spent their entire careers trying to overcome objections have suddenly and surprisingly found that sales come much easier, and they can make more sales in less time when they stop wasting time trying to convince non-buyers to buy. If you haven't let go of the overcoming objection idea yet, give it a try. The odds are that you too will achieve higher productivity, easier sales, and more and greater success!

Chapter 18

$

Finding Customers Verses Creating Customers

"If you give a man a fish, you've fed him for a day. But if you teach him how to fish, he'll patronize your bait shop."

I can't think of a single company where there are literally more buyers among the population than there are non-buyers. (Maybe Microsoft, but that's about it.)

Whatever you sell, it's natural to accept that most of the 300 million plus people living in the USA (and beyond for anyone selling outside the USA) will not want to buy your product or service, at least not from you, for many good reasons. This is why qualifying a prospect before you invest time, effort, and money into them is so important.

For example, it's not reasonable, nor rational for that matter, for a Corvette salesperson to target 16 year old drivers living in low income areas. Anything is possible in this world, but I think you get the point, don't you?

Most every product or service has a niche market with demographically targeted prospects. The people who exist outside of this target zone don't want or can't afford to buy from you, no matter how compelling your sales efforts may be. At least not in enough numbers to make pitching to them commercially viable.

However, salespeople and leaders of sales organizations who are imaginative sometimes look for and discover ways to create new customers for their products and services.

The tremendous advantage of doing this is that the people who'll become these new customers are not currently on your competitor's radar as prospects, so you're sales efforts go uncontested. Additionally, the loyalty that results from your company being the first one of its type to serve these new customers will cement the relationship for many years to come.

An obvious case study could include just about any franchise corporation. Take Kentucky Fried Chicken, for example. It started out with Colonel Sanders going from restaurant to restaurant, selling them on his unique recipe for frying chicken. This delicious recipe increased sales for these restaurants, but it also turned the restaurants into customers for the Colonel's pressure cookers, raw chicken, and batter ingredients. This became the foundation for his Kentucky Fried Chicken restaurant chain.

We've all witnessed the collapse of the US textile industry. Yet among the rubble exists a company that discovered a way to sell rags (yes, rags!) to laundries for the purpose of renting them out to other companies. The rags are used, than sent back to the rental company to be laundered and sent out again. By bringing this "rag rental" business model to the laundries, the textile company created a new revenue stream for the laundries, and extremely loyal new customers for themselves.

Finding a way to turn otherwise non-buyers into loyal customers can be done, and you can do it if you make doing so a priority and then set aside some study and thinking time. Keep your mind open to possibilities and tune your mental radar to seek out opportunities. You'll find that they'll come to you in good time.

Chapter 19

$

A True Story

One evening as Albert Einstein was being driven to give a lecture, he mentioned to his chauffeur, a man who somewhat resembled Einstein, that he was tired of speechmaking.

"I have an idea, boss," his chauffeur said, "I've heard you give this speech so many times, I'll bet I could give it for you."

Einstein laughed loudly and said, "Why not? Let's do it!"

When they arrived, Einstein donned the chauffeur's cap and jacket and sat in the back of the room. The chauffeur gave a beautiful rendition of Einstein's speech and even answered a few questions expertly.

Then a supremely pompous professor asked an extremely esoteric question, digressing here and there to let everyone in the audience know how brilliant he was. Without missing a beat, the chauffeur fixed the professor with a steely stare and said, "Sir, the answer to that question is so simple and so obvious that I will let my chauffeur, who is sitting in the back, answer it for me."

Many years ago, a rather ordinary looking couple came to Boston to meet with the president of Harvard University. They did not have an appointment, and were told that he was too busy to meet with them, but instead of leaving, they patiently waited to see him.

After a long wait, it became apparent to the president that they were not going to leave until he exchanged some words with them, so he finally agreed to give them a few moments of his time.

The couple took the opportunity to explain to the president that their son had attended Harvard for one year, and that he had cherished his time there, but he has since died as a result of an accident and they wanted to erect a memorial to him on the Harvard campus.

Unmoved by their story, the president explained to them that he didn't think such a landmark was appropriate on the property of so great an institution as Harvard University, and that perhaps they could locate their little memorial elsewhere. They responded by suggesting to him that perhaps the memorial could be in the form of a new building.

Observing their unremarkable appearance and annoyed by their naiveté, the president impatiently informed them that the Harvard campus contained over seven million dollars in buildings and equipment, and that the cost for them to erect such a memorial would be prohibitive.

Having finally been convinced by the university president that Harvard was not the place to memorialize their son, the couple left Boston. But they didn't give up on their idea, and they did erect a memorial to their son. It still exists today, and you can find it in Palo Alto, California, because when Mr. and Mrs. Leland Stanford realized that it *only* cost around seven million dollars to build an entire university, they decided that rather than adding to the Harvard campus, they would simply build one of their own, and so they did.

"You can easily judge the character of others by how they treat those who can do nothing for them or to them."
Malcolm Forbes

Chapter 20

$

A Not So True Story

A local business was looking for a sales person. They put a sign in the window saying: "SALES PERSON WANTED. Must be able to type, must be good with a computer and must be bilingual. We are an Equal Opportunity Employer."

A short time afterwards, a dog trotted up to the window, saw the sign and went inside. He looked at the receptionist and wagged his tail, then trotted over to the sign, took it into his mouth and set it on the floor at her feet. Getting the idea, the receptionist got the sales manager. The sales manager looked at the dog and was surprised, to say the least. However, the dog looked determined, so he led him into the sales office.

Inside, the dog jumped up on the chair and stared at the manager. The manager said, "I can't hire you. The sign says you have to be able to type."

The dog jumped down, went to the typewriter and proceeded to type out a sample sales order. He took out the page and trotted over to the manager and gave it to him, then jumped back on the chair.

The manager was stunned, but then told the dog, "The sign says you have to be good with a computer."

The dog jumped down again and went to the computer. Climbing up on the chair, he proceeded to demonstrate his expertise with the contact management software and even produced a sample sales bid for several of the company's products and presented them to the manager. By this time the manager was totally dumbfounded! He looked at the dog and said, "I realize that you are a very intelligent dog and have some interesting abilities, however, I still can't give you the job."

The dog jumped down and went to the sign and put his paw on the part about being an Equal Opportunity Employer. The manager said, "Yes, but the sign also says that you have to be bilingual."

The dog looked the manager straight in the eye and said, "Meow."

Chapter 21

$

Getting Your Foot In The Door

A sales rep was selling his wares door to door. He knocked on the door of a woman who absolutely hated sales people of every kind, and she proceeded to make him very aware of this fact, reading him the riot act. Finally, upon completion, she slammed the door in his face.

At least, she thought she did, but to her surprise, the door did not close. Instead, it bounced back open. This intensified her already foul disposition.

Slamming it even harder, the door again bounced back open. Now she was beside herself with rage! Convinced that the salesman was blocking the door with his shoe, she stepped back to get a running start so as to slam the door hard enough to break his foot.

Just as she was about to launch herself at the door, the salesman spoke up. "Ma'am," he said rather urgently, "before you do that again, you might want to remove your cat."

Have you ever seen people who you knew would buy from you if you could just get your foot in the door, if you could just get your message to them on a favorable basis? I refer to this as the brother-in-law factor.

Notice how quickly people change once they realize that you're selling something. Often, their mind slams shut like a steel trap, and so they never hear your message. You've seen it, haven't you? Yet, if you could approach them as you would a brother-in-law, you know, just stop by the house, sit down on the couch while you're sharing a drink and maybe watching a game on TV, and just casually say, "By the way, I saw something the other day that made me think of you. It looked like something that you would really want."

They'd probably listen to the whole story, wouldn't they?

Traditional selling tries to teach you to persuade people to buy regardless of how closed their minds may be. In fact, traditional selling is like using a crowbar, with "rebuttals" for overcoming objections and such, they're attempting to give you tools for prying open people's minds so you can persuade them to buy.

For example, say there were 10 people who could use your product. Let's also suppose that all ten of them are going to buy from someone soon. You pitch all ten but not all of them buy. Why not?

There are probably many reasons, but it really doesn't matter, because the overriding problem is that they probably never really heard your message, did they?

It's as if you were pitching these people from outside the door, and the ones that didn't buy, well, they never really heard your message because their door was slammed shut, otherwise they would probably have bought, wouldn't they? After all, they're qualified prospects. They need and want your product, and they're going to buy it from someone soon, right?

Fortunately, some of them left the door open, didn't they?

At least a crack.

You see, so many salespeople are pitching their prospects from outside the door. What we need to do is find out if the door is open a crack first, so that our message won't be wasted.

I'm not talking about attempting to pry it open ourselves, I'm talking about simply identifying the condition of the door.

The essence of this principle is not attempting to open a closed mind, but to only invest your time, effort, and

76

money on those minds that are already open, at least a little.

So it all really comes down to persuading vs. sorting.

Rather than trying to turn a "no" into a "yes," look for more yeses. They're out there, if you just take the time to look for them. But you can't find the yeses if you're too busy trying to turn someone's no into a yes.

Just remember, if you seek, you *will* find.

Chapter 22

$

Negotiating Tip Number One:
Be Very Clear

In the early days following the communist revolution in Russia, a particularly enthusiastic Bolshevik named Rudolph was having a discussion with his new bride. Commenting on the weather, she told him that she hoped it would soon stop snowing.

"That's not snow, darling, it's rain." He told her.

"You're wrong, Rudy, it's snow." She replied.

"No, honey, that's rain. It's raining outside." Rudy said, trying to remain civil.

"No, Rudy, it's snow!" she argued.

Back and forth they went until Rudy could take it no longer. Straining to contain his frustration, he blurted out, "It's rain! Trust me, I know what I'm talking about! Rudolph the red knows rain, dear!"

When you communicate, especially when negotiating, how clearly is your message understood by the other party? Have you thought about what it is like to be on the receiving end of your communication, and how much of what you are saying is being heard?

If you assume that your message is getting through, consider this: A landmark study of the "miscomprehension" of 25 typical TV commercials revealed that all of them were miscomprehended by the viewers to some extent. Up to 40 percent of the audience did not understand the meaning of the message, with the BEST commercials having no better than 81 percent viewer comprehension.

Can you guess why? What can we learn from this information, and how can it help you?

For starters, we know that in developing those commercials–which were studied and rated by focus groups–communication experts spent days or weeks, in some cases months, working out every word and syllable that would be heard or read by viewers.

Individuals who specialize in the art of delivering a persuasive message worked together as a team to see to it that everything was exactly right. In addition, they had the benefit of powerful visual tools and techniques at their disposal. In the end, however, at least 19 percent of the people who viewed their messages were confused.

What about *your* message?

What do you suppose is the comprehension level of your audience without the power of visual aids, animation, colors, lights and music all working for you? Is there a chance that your audience will miscomprehend what you are trying to say, and if they do, how persuasive can you be within this environment?

Since you can't possibly put as much time and attention into communicating your idea as producers of TV commercials put into theirs, it is important to realize that there is a very high probability that your message may be misunderstood by the recipient.

Extensive studies have revealed that top negotiators are much more clearly understood than average negotiators. They recognize how easy it is for others to make an incorrect inference, so they work extra hard to prevent that from occurring.

How do they do it, and how can you do it too?

Be clear. Be very clear. Know that you are being clear by getting feedback from your prospects. This lets you know not only what you think you have communicated, but also what they have understood from what you have said.

Communicate one idea at a time. Keep in mind: different people think differently. They think and hear based upon their frame of reference, not yours. When you communicate your message, be predisposed to saying it in multiple ways. As E. B. White stated: "When you say something, make sure you have said it. The chances of your having said it are only fair."

And finally, keep it simple. Quoting E. B. White again, "Let every word tell."

Negotiating Tip Number One: Be Very Clear.

Chapter 23

$

Negotiating Tip Number Two:
Avoid Counter Proposals

One fine summer day, a particularly mediocre salesman had just closed his second deal in two weeks, and he was feeling pretty good about the world. Thinking about how he closed those deals, he was also feeling pretty clever.

He decided that now would be a good time to close another deal…with the *big man* upstairs. Looking to heaven, he asked, "Lord, how much is a million years to you?"

Instantly, a booming voice from above replied, "Oh, about a second."

Not at all surprised to receive such a quick response to his question, the salesman continued, "And how much is a million dollars to you?"

Again, the reply was immediate, "Oh, about a penny," God responded.

"Ah ha," thought the salesman, "this is going to be easier than I thought."

Feeling full of confidence and self satisfaction, the salesman went for the close, "Lord, can I have a penny?"

"Sure you can," replied the Lord, "just a second!"

Have you ever presented an idea to a person or a group, only to have someone immediately present a different solution or idea? How did it make you feel to have your idea countered without even a discussion? Did it make you want to accept their idea?

This feeling of rejection is exactly what you *don't* want your prospect to feel. It causes them to become uncomfortable, and hurts your ability to be perceived as caring about the other party's problems. It also triggers a defensive reaction which causes them to become very creative in finding reasons why their idea or argument is valid, and this makes them own their idea even more, turning a simple difference into an emotional battle.

A study of top and average negotiators has revealed that the masters rarely if ever offer up a counter proposal immediately, while the average negotiators were much more likely to do so. The expert negotiators understand that doing this will harm their credibility, for they know that to sell to someone, it is vitally important that they believe that you care about helping them solve their problem. Countering someone's offer or proposal without first working through the elements of it tends to be perceived as a lack of appreciation for that person's situation, which is detrimental to getting agreement.

If someone does offer an idea which you feel is not workable, or perhaps their idea triggers an even better one in your mind, resist the temptation to counter their argument. Work through what they have presented first. Ask them questions about areas that you feel may not work, or can be improved upon. Rather than saying, "I don't see how this would work," ask them, "How exactly would this work?" Let them discover for themselves a better way, and they will be much more likely to accept it.

Always explore someone else's idea with them before offering an alternative.

Negotiating Tip Number Two: Avoid Counter Proposals.

Chapter 24

$

Negotiating Tip Number Three: Never Dilute Arguments

Bob: "At my house, I always have the last word."
Joe: "Oh really, what do you say?"
Bob: "Yes, dear."

Among the secrets of the world's top negotiators, one technique stands out: The idea of never diluting your argument.

Specifically, I am referring to giving your opponent additional reasons for agreeing with your point. On the surface, it would seem that giving someone more reasons to agree with you would strengthen your position, however, research shows that expert negotiators don't try to add reasons because doing so tends to dilute rather than strengthen the argument. Bombarding the other side with additional reasons to agree with you tends to make your argument weaker rather than stronger.

Since selling is very much a negotiation, professional salespeople can learn a lot from this discovery.

For example: A prospect states that he doesn't agree with the salesperson's estimate of how much money he might save as a result of buying and using the salesperson's product. The salesperson then begins to provide additional facts or reasons to back up his cost savings claim. Since it's natural to use your most compelling facts first, each fact or reason given is always weaker than the one preceding it. Finally, the salesperson offers up a really weak reason, and the prospect dismantles that reason and along with it goes the sale.

Expert negotiators–as well as top salespeople–don't feel the need to build their case with additional arguments or points that may weaken their overall position. They don't fall into the trap of providing a weak argument simply because the other side is demanding more reasons.

Instead, the most successful negotiators have found that focusing on the reason for the disagreement, rather than trying to defend their argument, is the best way to make real progress.

In our previous example, instead of offering more facts or reasons for his argument, if the salesperson instead asks some questions about why the prospect feels the way he does, specifically how important the cost savings factor really is to the prospect, the sales process may very likely have a completely different result. Perhaps cost savings isn't even the prospect's primary reason for wanting the product. If that is true, then giving additional facts or reasons about that component would be moot if not a complete deal killer.

Don't fall into the trap of offering additional reasons to back up your argument just because someone appears to disagree with you. Instead, ask questions to get to the heart of the true reason for the disagreement. What you learn may surprise you, and will definitely help you to better serve your prospects and clients far into the future.

Negotiating Tip Number Three: Never Dilute Arguments.

Chapter 25

$

Negotiating Tip Number Four:
Avoid Irritators

Harry and Janice were preparing to celebrate their 50th wedding anniversary. Harry had wanted to do something really special for Janice, but unfortunately, his pension was just enough to pay the bills, so he instead had to plan on a modest dinner and a movie.

That evening, when Harry announced his plans, Janice took him by the hand and lead him into the bedroom. Reaching into the closet, she removed an old shoebox from the top shelf and opened it. Looking inside, Harry saw five doilies and stacks of cash totaling over a hundred thousand dollars.

Janice explained, "When we first got married, my mother told me that to stay in love with you, I should crochet a doily every time you did something that irritated me."

"I'm amazed that I've only irritated you five times in fifty years." Harry said. "But where did you get all that money?"

"I made those five doilies yesterday," she said. "The money came from selling all the other doilies at fifty cents each."

There's a phrase you'll rarely if ever hear a top negotiator say, because it has such a negative impact on a negotiation. It's the term "generous offer," i.e. "I'm making you a very generous offer."

How do you usually feel when you're on the receiving end of that statement?

If you're like most people, you probably feel irritated. I don't blame you, which is why those words, and others like them, should be avoided when negotiating–or selling–your position to another person or a group of people.

Another irritator to avoid is the word "fair," as in, "Our offer is a very fair one."

Likewise, the word "reasonable" should be avoided.

Using words such as fair, reasonable, and generous imply that the other party is being the opposite. If I'm being fair, then you're being unfair. If I'm being reasonable, then you're being unreasonable.

Benjamin Franklin discovered this principle, and learned to express himself in modest terms. As he put it, "Never using when I advance any thing that may possibly be disputed, the words, "certainly," "undoubtedly," or any others that give the air of positiveness to an opinion."

Irritators are words or phrases that evoke a negative emotional response from the person to whom they are directed. It's like pressing a button that hits a nerve. Some people like to use them to tweak their opponent, but experts know better. Top negotiators avoid using irritators.

Perhaps a quick analysis of the words you use ought to be made before you undertake your next sale or negotiation. Try to identify those words that irritate you when you are on the receiving end, and work to eliminate them from your vocabulary.

Negotiating Tip Number Four: Avoid Irritators.

Chapter 26

$

Being Proactive in the
Selling Business

At a fabric store, a pretty girl spotted some nice material for a dress and asked the male sales clerk how much it cost.

"Only one kiss per yard," he replied with a smile.

"That's fine," she said, "I'll take ten yards."

The sales clerk excitedly measured out the cloth, wrapped it up, and then teasingly held it out. The girl took the bag and, pointing to the old woman standing beside her, said, "Grandma will pay the bill."

The title selected for this chapter may seem obvious, but please read on...it's about more than you might think at first glance.

Unless you're a professional order taker–and I doubt you'd be reading this if you were–you understand that business is not just going to come to you, you have to *do* something to get it. For this reason, we are all aware of the importance of being "proactive" in the selling business.

Prospecting, advertising, promoting, networking–these are all terms that refer to a form of getting your message out, making others aware of who you are and what you're selling. Obviously, you have to do some of these activities in order to sell your product or service, and it is probably this type of activity that you think of when you hear the term "proactive" with regards to selling.

But I'm not referring to this particular definition of proactive. In fact, I think that to devote an entire chapter to something as obvious as that would be a waste of your valuable time and an insult to your intelligence.

There is a particular sales trainer who bills himself as one of the best. He's written several books, and he runs expensive training workshops. Several years ago I read in one of his books how, after salespeople or their employers had shelled out a lot of money to attend one of his training sessions, he tells his students that if they want to sell more, they must make 10 more calls before they go home each day. He then goes on to calculate the numbers to demonstrate how this would amount to an additional 2,500 additional calls per year, which will add up to many more appointments, many more sales and most importantly, many more commission dollars.

He also mentions that often his attendees, upon hearing this, will become upset, and some will actually walk out because they feel that they don't need to pay someone to tell them something they already know.

He then goes on to explain how these people who are disgruntled or who walk out are losers, because there is nothing really new in selling, and they just need to be reminded of how things really are. I suppose he feels that he's giving them a dose of "tough love."

But if you think about it, the idea of simply working harder is not only so obvious as to almost be insulting, it's actually counter productive. After all, successful sales people are usually already working very hard, maybe too hard, which is the very reason for their seeking new ways to work smarter in the first place. Simply putting more time in doesn't lead to higher productivity. Time is, after all, our most valuable asset, for you can never get more of it, and you can never get it back once it's gone.

No, the answer is not to work longer or harder. You can do these things if you choose, but that kind of message is not likely to inspire or motivate anyone, it just tends to disappoint people who are honestly seeking a *better way*.

And there IS a better way. I believe that no matter how well you do something, there's *always* a better way. And you *will* find it if you never stop seeking it. Even the Bible states, "Seek and you shall find."

The message here is to be proactive in seeking a better way to do whatever it is you are doing.

Thomas Edison invented a way of recording sounds on a cylinder so they could be played back later. It was amazing, but someone else believed that there was an even better way to do it. Along came vinyl LPs, then magnetic tape, then laser discs, then digital. Is this as good as it will ever get, or is there still a better way yet to do it?

Samuel Morse developed a method for communicating messages across long distances over a wire. But Guglielmo Marconi believed there was a better way, and gave us radio. Radio waves lead to microwaves, analog signals lead to digital, copper wire lead to optical fibers, and on it goes. There's always a better way, isn't there?

The old saying, "Don't fix what isn't broke," may seem like wisdom to some, but if everyone took it to heart, we'd still be cooking our meals over an open fire, wouldn't we?

And never underestimate the advantage that even a slight improvement can give you, because you don't have to work twice as hard as everyone else to be the leader. Just staying one step ahead of the competition puts you out in front.

I believe that people who are satisfied to just work longer or harder are like the gazelle. They will end up running very fast, faster in fact than almost every other animal, but they're still running away. But those people who continually seek to improve their results with better ideas are like the cheetah. They're running toward something with purpose, not away from something in fear.

And never forget–to survive, the gazelle has to outrun the fastest cheetah, but the cheetah only has to outrun the slowest gazelle.

Chapter 27

$

Seinfeld on Marketing

"Why is it when you turn on the TV you see ads for telephone companies, and when you turn on the radio you hear ads for TV shows, and when you get put on hold on the phone you hear a radio station? And did you see these new minivan ads? All they talk about are cup holders, kiddie seats, and doors. What kind of advertising is that? When you see an ad for a suit, do they say, "And look at the zipper! Carefully hidden, but easily accessible when you need it!" I think not!"

- Jerry Seinfeld

In 1998, when the sitcom *Seinfeld* went off the air, it was the top rated TV show in the US, joining *I Love Lucy* and *The Andy Griffith Show* as the only three TV shows in history to end their runs at the top of the US ratings. At the time, the network was offering Jerry Seinfeld the sum of five million dollars *per episode* to continue the show for another season, which he declined to do.

Yet, just a few years before, the show had not even been among the top 30 in the ratings, the critics gave it no chance, and the network executives were demanding that the supporting cast be scrapped.

So what caused such a dramatic turn around? The answer lies in the direction the writers decided to take in the fourth season.

Up until that time, the show really didn't have a clear identity. But in season four, the writers decided to have the characters Jerry and George write a pilot for a sitcom which would be titled *Jerry*. This was, of course, a parallel to the actual show *Seinfeld*.

In the story, the show *Jerry* would be a show about nothing. This was the gag of the story. Yet somehow this gag extended to the actual *Seinfeld* series, and almost overnight, *Seinfeld* became known as the show about "nothing."

Suddenly, *Seinfeld* had an identity, a niche. It was the show about nothing. It now had an articulated position among the other sitcoms, and this generated interest.

With the same actors and the same writers doing basically the same quality of work, the show suddenly become very popular due to the fact that it now had established a position in the minds of the viewers. Seinfeld didn't get better overnight, but its ratings did.

Seven Up positioned itself as the "uncola" and overnight catapulted itself as the number one non-cola soft drink. Seven Up's lemon lime flavor didn't get better after they positioned themselves as the uncola, but their sales sure did.

Avis positioned itself as the company that "tries harder" because it is number two in the car rental business.

Wendy's used its *Where's the Beef* campaign to position itself as the fast food restaurant that served really big hamburgers.

Present yourself, your product, or your company in such a way that you occupy a position in the minds of the people whom you are trying to reach. Just as Seinfeld became known as the show about nothing, you must become known for something.

Positioning yourself *will* make a difference.

Chapter 28

$

Why Adversity is Your Best Friend

A salesman hobbled in to his house and was greeted by his wife. "Dear," she said, startled, "what are you doing home so early?"

"The boss and I had a fight," he grumbled. "He wouldn't take back what he said."

Glowing with pride, his wife asked, "what did he say?"

"You're fired."

Within every adversity is the seed to an equal or greater benefit. So stated W. Clement Stone, time and time again. And he ought to have known, for he built an insurance empire during the great depression.

Within every adversity IS the seed to an equal or greater benefit.

Don't believe it? Consider this:

A study of successful business owners revealed that of all the things to which they attributed their success, the number one reason they listed was losing a job.

Most people would consider getting laid off, fired, or otherwise losing their job to be a major adversity. How about you?

Yet, more often than not, successful people consider having lost a job to have been one of the best things to have happened to them, although they were probably somewhat less than exuberant about it at the time.

In the late 1970's, Lee Iacocca was president of the Ford Motor Company and the largest shareholder of Ford stock outside of the Ford family. Yet at that time most Americans not involved with the auto industry didn't know who Lee Iacocca was. Then, one day, suddenly and for no apparent reason, Henry Ford II fired Lee. It was as much of a surprise to Iacocca as it was to the rest of the world. And to add insult to injury, all of Iacocca's associates and friends within the Ford organization had been warned by Henry Ford to have no contact with him– or else! In addition to being perplexed, Iacocca found himself ashamed and alone. The weeks immediately following his firing were very dark days for Lee. Iacocca was once quoted as saying, "It's a good thing that God doesn't let you see your future, or you might be sorely tempted to shoot yourself."

Of course, we all know the rest of the story. Chrysler was in dire need of someone to turn things around, and Iacocca was now available, so he took the job. Just a few short years from the darkest times of his life, Iacocca became a hero among business executives and blue collar working people alike. His autobiography topped the best seller list, and many people were even calling for Iacocca to run for president. His became one of the most famous and respected names among business executives around the world! And all because he lost a job!

Still having doubts? Consider the following:

A woman survived the attacks on 9/11 because her alarm clock didn't go off in time. Another survived as a result of being late for work because of being stuck on the New Jersey Turnpike as a result of an auto accident. Another person survived because he missed his bus. Someone else was spared because she spilled food on her clothes and had to take time to change. Another person missed a date with disaster because his car wouldn't start. One had a child that dawdled and didn't get ready as soon as he should have. One couldn't get a taxi. Then there was the man who put on a new pair of shoes that morning, and on the way to work developed a blister on his foot, so he stopped at a drugstore to buy a Band-Aid.

Within every adversity *is* the seed to an equal or greater benefit.

Chapter 29

$

A Tip for Sales Managers

Having trouble motivating sales reps? Perhaps the following idea will help.

We all know how a person's self image can affect their performance, and negative sales results only feed a negative self image. Here's how new or struggling sales reps can get a real boost with a simple technique.

Imagine that Sam is a struggling sales rep, and we give him a list of one hundred prospects, and task him with selling ten of the people on his list.

Between a negative self image and bad luck, it is likely that Sam will fall far short of his goal, resulting in him ending the day on a bad note, and going home feeling defeated, which will negatively affect his performance the following day.

But even if Sam were to sell ten that day, his negative self image might tell him that he was just lucky, because that list could easily have contained fewer names who might buy. Selling involves negative swings, after all.

On the other hand, what if Sam was given that same list and instructed to disqualify at least ninety prospects? Unlike making ten sales, which is a goal that bad luck or poor performance could prevent, disqualifying ninety prospects is a behavior that is totally within Sam's control.

Now suppose he comes back to you and says that he was able to disqualify ninety five prospects? You could say, mission accomplished! Sam did his job and made five sales besides. You can send Sam home feeling good about his performance. Luck was not a factor in accomplishing the task he was given, and Sam knows this.

Alternatively, if Sam comes to you and says, "I was only able to disqualify eighty eight prospects because twelve wanted to buy, then you simply give Sam a few more prospects to contact until he disqualifies ninety. And when Sam goes home, he will again feel great about his performance, because he accomplished his goal plus he made twelve sales.

Using this process of assigning your people goals that they can easily control, such as disqualifying, you can guarantee that every sales rep hits their goal 100% of the time, as long as they are not lazy or completely unsuited to be working with people. Then it just becomes a matter of helping them to gradually increase their sales skills and abilities, but you will find that this is much easier to do this with a person who has a positive self image rather than a negative one.

Chapter 30

$

The Single Most Important
Selling Skill Part I

Perhaps the single most important skill necessary for successful selling to all types of people is what we refer to as versatility. Being versatile enough to adapt your behavior style to your prospect's style will go a long way to helping them feel more comfortable with you, which helps lower the defensive walls most prospects have.

Although a single person's behavior can change dramatically depending upon the situation and their role in it, most people tend to have a default style, one that they naturally revert to when they are just being themselves. Sometimes this style is not the one that you see when they are in the prospect or customer mode. This is why extreme care must be taken when attempting to evaluate and identify a person's style.

Many books have been written about "personality types" and the like, promising to transform the reader into a Sigmund Freud of sorts, implying that if the reader masters the set of skills offered up by the author, they will somehow receive the power to psychoanalyze their target to determine just how to be in control of the prospect and reduce them to mere putty in their hands.

This idea fails to appreciate just how complex people are. If it takes professional analysts who are experts on human behavior months or even years of therapy to get a handle on a person's motivations and how to work with them, how can we hope to do it in a few minutes? The answer is, of course, we can't.

What we *can* do is to observe the *behavior* of our prospects and deal with that. Don't try to second guess the why behind what you observe, just deal with the behavior at face value. It is what it is. Then, adapt yourself to mirror the behavior you observe. There is nothing "phony" in doing this, it is simply being the professional in the relationship. You expect other professionals to alter their behavior to suit their profession, why would selling be any different?

Chapter 31

$

The Single Most Important
Selling Skill Part II

Identifying the specific behavior style of your prospect will help you appeal to what he or she wants in the manner that he or she is most comfortable receiving it. This reduces the typical defensive posture of prospects and results in more and easier sales.

It is fairly easy to observe the degree to which a prospect is assertive and responsive. Doing so allows you to identify four behavior extremes which can be labeled. You can then categorize a person's behavior as one among four behavior styles.

Before we look at these styles, let's first identify what we mean by assertiveness and responsiveness. Assertiveness refers to how much a person tries to take control of the conversation. One example of this is the idea that people who interrupt are more assertive than those who do not.

Responsiveness refers to how much a person responds to what others say and do. For example, someone who asks questions about what you have said would be more responsive than someone who seems to ignore what you have just said and states or asks about something else, as though they are changing the subject.

The four extremes, with the corresponding label in parentheses, would represent people who are very assertive and very responsive (Engaging), very assertive and non-responsive (Commanding), non-assertive and very responsive (Caring), and non-assertive and non-responsive (Studying). These labels more or less describe what a casual observer might assume the person is doing based on the behavior that that is displayed, but keep in

101

mind that their underlying motivations for the behavior you observe may not necessarily match the label. They may be non-assertive and non-responsive for reasons that have nothing to do with studying the situation. The label is simply to make it easier to identify the category. We are not concerned about their motives, but rather the behavior that we are observing.

Also, note that we are talking about extremes. A person's behavior will most often not be at either extreme end of the scale for low or high assertiveness, and low or high responsiveness, but will instead fall somewhere in between.

Identifying a person's assertiveness and responsiveness and then labeling that behavior will help you to know how to adjust your behavior to help them to be more comfortable with you, which will automatically reduce their resistance.

If a prospect speaks softly, doesn't interrupt you, and willingly and readily provides feedback about what you are saying, then that person would be labeled "Caring." He or she may not care any more about your product or service than anyone exhibiting the other behavior styles, but knowing that they are nonassertive and responsive allows you to know how to adjust your behavior to match them and make them feel more comfortable with you. Using the "Caring" label simply makes it easier to remember and respond to their behavior style.

The reasons this works are many and complex, but the simple answer is that the more you act like your prospect, the more they believe that they can predict your behavior, which reduces tension and puts them more at ease.

Using this concept and implementing it in the selling arena has helped many salespeople become top producers in a very short time, and applying this skill will enhance your sales results also.

Chapter 32

$

To Err is Human

The next time you make a mistake, you can take heart when you reflect on what follows. After you read these gems, I'll bet you won't feel so bad about your own blunders:

"There is no likelihood man can ever tap the power of the atom."

Robert Millikan, Nobel Physicist

"Email is not to be used to pass on information or data. It should be used only for company business."

Accounting Manager, Electric Boat Company

"This project is so important, we can't let things that are more important interfere with it."

UPS Advertising/Marketing Mgr

"Teamwork is a lot of people doing what I say."

Marketing executive, Citrix Corporation

"My sister passed away and her funeral was scheduled for Monday. When I told my boss, he said she died so that I would have to miss work on the busiest day of the year. He then asked if we could change her burial to Friday. He said, "That would be better for me."

Shipping Executive, FTD Florists

"We know that communication is a problem, but the company is not going to discuss it with the employees."

AT&T Lone Lines Division

"One day my boss asked me to submit a status report to him concerning a project I was working on. I asked him if tomorrow would be soon enough. He said, "If I wanted it

103

tomorrow, I would have waited until tomorrow to ask for it!"

New Business Manager, Hallmark Cards

"640K ought to be enough for anybody"

Bill Gates, Microsoft

"As of tomorrow, employees will only be able to access the building using individual security cards. Pictures will be taken next Wednesday and employees will receive their cards in two weeks."

Fred Dales at Microsoft Corporation

"Well informed people know it is impossible to transmit the voice over wires and that were it possible to do so, the thing would be of no practical value."

The Boston Post

"There is no need for any individual to have a computer in their home."

Ken Olson, President of
Digital Equipment Corporation

"I think there is a world market for maybe five computers."

Thomas Watson, Founder of IBM

"So we went to Atari and said, 'Hey, we've got this amazing thing, even built with some of your parts, and what do you think about funding us? Or we'll give it to you. We just want to do it. Pay our salary, we'll come work for you.' And they said, 'No.' So then we went to Hewlett-Packard, and they said, 'Hey, we don't need you. You haven't got through college yet.'"

Steve Jobs

Chapter 33

$

The Power of the Interrogative?

Do you mind if I ask you a few quick questions?

- Why don't you ever see the headline *Psychic Wins Lottery*?
- Why is it that to stop Windows, you have to click on *Start*?
- Why is lemon juice made with artificial flavor, and dishwashing liquid made with real lemons?
- If it's true that we're here to help others, then what are the others here for?
- If quitters never win and winners never quit, why are we told to quit while we're ahead?
- If flying is so safe, why do they call the airport the terminal?
- Can orphans eat at a family restaurant?
- Why do we drive on a parkway and park on a driveway?

What *is* the power of the interrogative? Restated in a less stuffy manner, it's simply the power of asking questions, isn't it?

Would you like to have the power of the interrogative working for you?

If you understand something about conversation, and I have a good idea that you do, you know that asking questions is really the key to having leverage, or power, in a selling or negotiating situation, isn't it?

So should we, as sales professionals, ask questions? Should we ask questions often? Is it also correct to say that we should strive to ask the *right* questions?

This concept is simple enough, but what is the real purpose of asking all of these questions? Is it simply to acquire information? It would seem so, but that's not the only reason for asking questions, is it?

Are you aware that those who understand how to use questions as a powerful selling tool have different uses for asking them? Do you realize that inquiring for the purpose of gaining knowledge is only one of these many uses?

For example, how would you correctly complete this statement: "In fourteen hundred ninety two, Columbus sailed the ocean _____?"

If you're like everyone else who has ever been asked this question, you answered "blue," didn't you? Unfortunately, did you suspect that you are not even close? The correct answer is, of course, "to find an alternative ocean route to the far east," isn't that right?

Don't feel bad, because "blue" *is* the obvious answer, isn't it?

You see, we tend to assume the obvious, don't we?

But you remember the joke about what happens when you "ass u me" don't you?

So being precise will avoid improper assumptions, won't it?

Did you know that one way of being precise is to always clarify by asking questions?

So one alternative use for asking questions would be to clarify our point, wouldn't it?

After you make your point, can you see how you could then make sure that your prospect clearly understands you by restating the point slightly differently, and in the form of a question?

Another purpose of asking questions is to direct the flow of the exchange, because the person who asks the questions is the person who's in control of the conversation, isn't that right?

There is tremendous power in asking questions, isn't there? It can help you to uncover your prospect's needs, to be sure, but do you realize that questions can also help you reveal your prospect's desires to himself (or herself)? And people will often do almost anything to get what they desire, including giving you their money in exchange for your product or service, won't they?

And did you also know that questions can be used as a stalling tactic? Does it surprise you to learn that expert negotiators will ask questions simply to tie up the other party's thinking while they use that time to improvise a new strategy?

Would you like to have the power of the interrogative working for you? Are you aware that every statement in this chapter was in the form of a question?

Maybe a little overkill, but you get the point...don't you?

Chapter 34

$

The Power of a
Positive Mental Attitude

A recently unemployed salesperson walked into the human resources department of a large sales organization and handed the executive her resume. As the executive scanned the document, the salesperson noticed several framed posters on the walls that featured beautiful scenic photographs, each accompanied by a statement mentioning the importance of "Attitude."

"I must say," stated the executive, "your work history is terrible. All of your previous jobs ended in termination."

"Yes," she replied, "but you'll notice at the top of the list of my strengths I listed Positive Attitude."

"Well," continued the executive, "there's not much positive in being fired from every job you've ever had."

"Yes, there is," responded the salesperson, "it proves that I'm not a quitter!"

W. Clement Stone is best known as the author of the books, *Success through a Positive Mental Attitude*, and *The Success System That Never Fails*, and the person who made famous the phrase, "Do It Now!" as well as having been the publisher of *SUCCESS Magazine*.

In 1939, Mr. Stone was managing a large national insurance agency that he had founded years earlier. He had over one thousand agents working for him across the country, but on this day while he was vacationing with his family in Florida, he received a telegram from the home office of the insurance company which his agency represented.

The telegram stated that in two weeks, his license to sell for them would be revoked, and neither he nor any of his hundreds of agents would be able to sell the company's insurance products anymore, and they would cease to receive renewal commissions at that time. The telegram also stated that the president of the insurance company was going on a trip overseas and would not be available for the next two months.

The type of license that he was going to lose was not being written anymore, so there was no other insurance company that he could transfer his business to in order to continue operations. This devastated Mr. Stone, as it would anyone facing such a crisis. He not only had his personal fortune at stake, but over a thousand salesmen depending on him, most with families to provide for. How could he deal with such a "no-win" situation? As he put it, "What do you do when the walls come crashing down?"

Rather than accepting the bad news, however, Mr. Stone decided to practice what he had been preaching and keep a positive attitude. He determined that his license would not be cancelled, and he also determined that he would form his own insurance company so that he would never again be at the mercy of corporate bigwigs.

After tracking down the insurance company's president, he worked out an arrangement to postpone the action until the president returned from his trip, at which time he worked out a compromise with the insurance company to keep his license in effect. But more importantly, he did start his own insurance company, Combined Insurance, and by 1954, it was the largest stock company in the USA selling accident insurance exclusively. Eventually, he built an insurance and financial empire that included the largest insurance brokerage in the world.

It has been said that attitude is more important than facts, than the past, than education, than money, than circumstances, than failures, than successes, than what other people think or say or do. It is more important than appearance, giftedness, or skill, and that life is 10 percent what happens *to* a person, and 90 percent how they choose to respond to it.

It's easy to think that you have a positive attitude when things are going well. The real test is when things go wrong. It's at that time you may need to have and *use* a positive attitude to avert a crisis. It's like owning a car that you never use. For years it will sit in the garage, but you had better keep it in good working order by maintaining it and taking it out on the road from time to time, otherwise when you need it, it may not work, and all the years of owing it will have been of no value to you.

The simple technique that Mr. Stone advocated was to repeat several times each day, in a loud voice, the following phrase: I feel happy, I feel healthy, I feel terrific!

In selling as in everyday life, a positive attitude will serve you in more ways than you can count. Mr. Stone is no longer with us, but he lived to age one hundred, and his advice will still be as valid one hundred years from now is it is today, so why not use this chapter as a reminder to check your attitude each day. If you find yourself becoming negative, determine at that moment that you are going to be positive in all circumstances, for it is in this way that you can successfully handle the tough times that come along, and make the good things in life come to you more quickly and easily.

Chapter 35

$

Seeing Is Believing

A Buddhist was walking down the street in New York City when he began to feel hungry. Approaching a hot dog cart, he asked the vendor for a hot dog. When the vendor asked him what he wanted on it, the Buddhist answered, "Make me one with everything."

Do you believe that a salesperson's self image can affect their performance? I surely do, because I witnessed amazing proof of it. Here's what happened:

A major catastrophe was about to befall a sales office staffed with thirty sales reps. The sole admin person whose job it was to process all the new orders for the office was feeling ill, and when she became too sick to work, a temporary replacement was unavailable. During the next four weeks, new sales were not processed as the paperwork piled up. When she finally returned to her job, she had about four weeks worth of sales orders waiting to be processed.

All month long she worked feverishly to process both the new sales orders coming in plus the backlogged orders, and all during that month, the wall chart that displayed the sales results for each of the reps began to reflect fantastic numbers as everyone watched their sales add up at twice the usual rate. They understood that those numbers did not accurately reflect the single month's production, nevertheless, day after day they saw those numbers sprint higher and higher, culminating in double the usual sales numbers for a given month.

Now for the rest of the story.

The effect of looking at double numbers on a sales chart had an amazing impact on the self image of those sales reps, because the following month, that sales chart again reflected production numbers double that of a typical month, except this time it was because the reps had legitimately doubled their production.

And this was not a lone incident. The higher sales performance became the new standard for that sales office, month after month.

It is true that seeing is believing. This statement has more power behind it than most people appreciate.

As a new and failing sales rep, I decided that I was going to stop the insanity and begin to succeed. Peter J. Daniels, the Australian businessman who inspired me, has told me about the power of the imagination, so I decided I would put mine to work for me. I took out my miserable paycheck, and stared at it, then closing my eyes, I saw that check in my mind, except the number I saw in my mind was not the number that appeared on the physical check. In my mind I saw a number much higher. Much, much higher. And I concentrated on this vision intensely, imagining that I have such a check now.

And in less than 60 days, I was holding my latest paycheck with that exact dollar amount printed on it.

It has been proven to me time and again that what a person believes is what he or she will receive. And seeing IS believing.

Chapter 36

$

An Outrageous Claim!

The following story first appeared in The Military Advocate, vol. VIII, no. 3: (1). The irony is great, and the retelling may make for a good ice breaker when meeting with a new prospect (unless he happens to be a lawyer).

A Charlotte, NC, lawyer purchased a box of very rare and expensive cigars, then insured them against fire among other things. Within a month, having smoked his entire stockpile of these great cigars and without yet having made even his first premium payment on the policy, the lawyer filed claim against the insurance company. In his claim, the lawyer stated the cigars were lost "in a series of small fires." The insurance company refused to pay, citing the obvious reason: that the man had consumed the cigars in the normal fashion.

The lawyer sued...and won!

In delivering the ruling the judge agreed with the insurance company that the claim was frivolous. The Judge stated nevertheless, that the lawyer held a policy from the company in which it had warranted that the cigars were insurable and also guaranteed that it would insure them against fire, without defining what is considered to be unacceptable fire, and was obligated to pay the claim.

Rather than endure a lengthy and costly appeal process, the insurance company accepted the ruling and paid $15,000 to the lawyer for his loss of the rare cigars.

Now for the best part...

After the lawyer cashed the check, the insurance company had him arrested on 24 counts of arson! With his own insurance claim and testimony from the previous case being used against him, the lawyer was convicted of intentionally burning his insured property and was sentenced to 24 months in jail and a $24,000 fine.

Chapter 37

$

The Awesome Power of a Useful Purpose

Junior was cooling his heels in the state prison and feeling quite depressed when he received a letter from his dad:

Dear Junior,

It looks like I won't be able to plant my garden this year. I'm just getting too old to be doing all that digging. If you were here, I know you'd turn the soil for me, and all my troubles would be over.

Love, Dad

A week later, the old man received a reply letter from his son:

Dad,

Whatever you do, *don't* dig up that garden! That's where the bodies are buried!

Junior

At four a.m. the next morning, scores of police showed up and dug up the entire area. Failing to find any bodies, they apologized to the old man and left. A few days later, the old man received another letter from his son:

Dad,

Go ahead and plant your garden now. It's the best I could do under the circumstances.

Junior

You know that Abraham Lincoln was president of the United States, but did you also know that he was a farmer, a clerk, a soldier, a lawyer, and a congressman as well? In fact, Mr. Lincoln worked successfully in many diverse professions, all with little or no formal education or training in his various fields of endeavor.

They say that necessity is the mother of invention, and Mr. Lincoln proved that it's also a powerful motivator for self development. "The little advance I now have upon this store of education," he said, "I have picked up from time to time under the pressure of necessity."

Mr. Lincoln was famous for being a clear writer and persuasive speaker, but he acknowledged that he learned little of this in school. "I could read, write, and cipher to the Rule of Three," he once admitted. His abilities in this area instead came to him as a result of offering to write letters for friends. This forced him to develop the skill of choosing the most effective words to successfully express what the letter writer wanted to say.

One of the skills Mr. Lincoln acquired early in his life was the art of surveying. As a young adult, he took a job as a surveyor, in spite of the fact that he had no surveying experience or training of any kind. He acquired two books on the subject and proceeded to study them day and night for six weeks. He also sought assistance in learning decimal fractions, the use of mathematical instruments, and the process for changing the scale of maps. As a result of his intensive self study, Mr. Lincoln quickly became known as an accurate surveyor who was more than once trusted to settle boundary disputes.

Abraham Lincoln discovered early in his career that the acquisition of knowledge for a specific, useful purpose can empower a person with the tremendous ability to focus attention and enhance concentration for prolonged periods. It was the combination of his varied skills, developed out of necessity and not by way of the formal education process, that lead Mr. Lincoln through the ranks of law and government, and ultimately into the oval office.

Study your profession, hone your craft, and never cease developing new skills. You never know where it may lead.

Chapter 38

$

Improved Selling Made Simple

A sales manager overheard a sales clerk saying to a customer, "No, we haven't had any for some weeks now, and it doesn't look as if we'll be getting any soon."

Alarmed, the manager rushed over to the customer who was walking out the door and said, "That isn't true, ma'am. Of course, we'll have some soon. In fact, we placed an order for it a couple of weeks ago."

Then the manager drew the sales clerk aside and growled, "Never, *ever* tell a customer that we don't have something. If we don't have it, say we ordered it and it's on its way. Now, what was it she inquiring about?"

"Rain."

I'm going to make a statement about selling that may seem strange to you, but please allow yourself a moment to consider exactly what is being stated:

No salesperson has ever washed out of selling because he failed to sell the people who would never buy.

Think about that for a moment.

No salesperson, not even the worst, most unpersuasive non-seller in existence, ever failed in the selling profession because he was unable to sell to non-buyers.

He may have failed for *attempting* to sell to non-buyers, but he never failed for not selling them.

When a salesperson fails, it's usually because he either lost the ones who would have bought by getting in the way of the deal, or because he didn't get himself in front of enough of the prospects who would buy.

Now, if you're a salesperson, it's extremely unlikely that you're the worst salesperson in the world, but it is likely that you're not quite as successful as you could be. There's always room for improvement, isn't there?

And the great thing about the selling profession is that when you improve, you see it directly in your paycheck.

So if you can improve, it stands to reason that your improvement in performance will come when you focus on one or more of the following three "landmines" which are: Spending too much time with non-buyers, getting in the way of a deal and preventing a potential buyer from buying, or not getting yourself in front of enough prospects who will buy.

Look, you know that there are only so many minutes in the day that you're willing to devote directly to selling. Everyone has their own personal tolerance for "face time" or "phone time." Whatever yours is, you want it to be as productive as possible, and every minute you spend with a non-buyer is costing you time, effort, and money.

For example, consider the performance of the top twenty percent of producers in your company or industry. What are their closing ratios? With few exceptions, most businesses have top producers that are closing fifty percent or less, usually well under fifty percent. In many industries, top producers may have closing rates as low as five to ten percent, yet they are their company's leaders and are enjoying a fantastic standard of living. So even top producers are spending more time with non-buyers than they want to, and if they had a proven method for identifying these non-buyers sooner, they would spend even less time with them, which would automatically make them more productive.

The second "landmine" getting in the way of the deal, can be the worst of the three because it is literally snatching defeat from the jaws of victory. Talking too much and buying your product back, not being sensitive to exactly what the prospect really wants, and failing to ask enough of the right questions to appear to care about the prospect's problems are three of the most common reasons that potential buyers change their minds and don't buy when they otherwise would have.

The third landmine has to do directly with time management. Spending too much time on non-selling activities leaves too little time to actually put yourself in front of potential buyers. Finding ways to eliminate non-essential, non-sales activities, and replacing them with ways to put yourself in front of more people who are predisposed to buying will result in more sales. Also, one of the biggest time wasters is the futile effort spent trying to sell to the non-buyers, which is the first landmine mentioned earlier.

Identify which of these landmines are costing you the most sales, and work to eliminate them. Then keep striving to improve your results. Eventually, you will experience higher productivity and more sales, and this is really what you want, isn't it?

Chapter 39

$

The Power of Motivation?

Life Insurance Salesman: "Don't let me frighten you into a decision. Sleep on it tonight, and *if* you wake up in the morning, let me know what you think."

There's a lot of talk about the need for motivation in a sales organization.

Many professional speakers bill themselves as "motivational speakers" and claim that they can speak on a huge range of subjects. Of course, they are not experts on all of these subjects, but rather, their expertise lies with their ability to give an interesting and entertaining speech which they custom to their audience by working in some facts and points about the subject of choice.

But many sales managers have complained that, although entertaining and somewhat helpful in the short term, these motivational talks don't really seem to produce any lasting improvements in performance. I understand their lament, because I believe that selling a motivational talk for its long term results is like selling a car wash under the guise of "preventative maintenance."

Motivational talks can help, but they're very much like a car wash. A car wash may provide a slight improvement in gas mileage for a short time, but it won't make the car run better, especially if there are problems under the hood. It will, however, extend the life of the finish and make the owner feel a little boost of pride immediately after getting one.

But is a short-lived shot of emotion the only result of motivation? It really depends on what *kind* of motivation we're talking about. The following is a contrast between

123

two kinds of motivation. Ask yourself which type of motivational boost you would rather receive.

Scenario 1: Picture hoards of warriors rallying to the exuberant speech of their commander as they prepare for battle. Between bouts of chanting and shouting, they listen intently as they are told how today they will taste victory. Raising and lowering his pitch and tone, altering inflection and pace as only a master motivator can, this charismatic leader keeps his people spellbound. He exhorts them, and tells them not to worry. "When you sight the enemy dogs through your rifles," he says, "the righteousness of your cause will cause the bullets to hit their marks."

With these and other inspirational words, this leader incites his people, whipping them into an emotional frenzy as he prepares to send most of them to their deaths. This is the power of motivation.

Scenario 2: Imagine well trained and disciplined soldiers sitting quietly as their commander briefs them. Their attitude is solemn and serious as they review how their stealth technology will allow them to remain invisible to the enemy as their sites will allow them to zero in on their targets through fog or smoke or blackness of night. He reminds them that their guided weapons will seek out and destroy their targets while they remain safely out of the range of the enemy's weapons. He reminds them that they have fought this battle countless times in training, and they know exactly what to do and how to do it. "Just remember your training," he tells them, "and you will successfully accomplish your mission."

This too is motivation, but a different kind of motivation. This is the motivation that comes with the confidence of knowing that you are prepared, and that you have the tools and the professional training to survive and to win.

Both types of motivation will move people to action. Which type do you want for your people?

Chapter 40

$

What Are Your Feelings?

Many years ago, an inquisitive reporter got an exclusive interview with Sigmund Freud, the famous psychiatrist. During the meeting, the reporter asked the doctor what process he used to make important decisions.

The father of psychoanalysis looked carefully at the reporter through his thick spectacles, and in his Austrian accent, told him that he always performed the same ritual in all his decision making.

The reporter leaned forward in anticipation, eager to learn his secret.

"I always flip a coin." He stated.

"You what?" the reporter cried. "You flip a coin? What kind of scientific method is that? How can you trust your most important decisions to chance?"

"Yes," Dr. Freud continued, "I always flip a coin. And then when I see what the result is, I ask myself how I feel about it."

Several years ago, Steve Irwin, the "Crocodile Hunter," was memorialized for days by the media around the world. He was mourned by millions of people far beyond his home nation of Australia, and if I were to ask a hundred people why he was so loved and admired by so many, I'll bet that nearly every one of them would give the same answer: He was so enthusiastic! He had passion for what he did, and he had the power of transferring his feelings to others through his unbounded exuberance.

Yes, enthusiasm sells! It's contagious. It's a powerful emotion that can easily be transferred to others.

I once heard one of the world's most successful salespeople give a really great definition of selling. He stated that selling is the transference of a feeling from one person to another. It's transferring *your* feelings about your product or service from you to your prospect. That's a pretty good definition of what selling is, I believe.

The question I have for you today is: What are *your* feelings about *your* product or service? If you were to transfer them to your prospect, would it be enough to motivate them to buy it?

I'm not talking about your feelings for wanting a sale, or a sales commission. I'm talking about your feelings about the product or service itself.

Just how do you really feel about what you sell?

The best test of this is to ask: Do you use your own product or service exclusively, or do you use your competition?

Now, don't get me wrong. I'm not one of those people who says that you *must* personally use your own product or service to sell it with integrity. I don't believe that at all.

The top salesperson for Raytheon who sells surface-to-surface missiles probably doesn't have one in his backyard pointed at his in-law's house. An x-ray machine salesperson most likely doesn't keep one in his basement to take family photos. And I rather doubt that the top salesperson for Huggies diapers wears them under his clothes on sales calls. There are all kinds of products and services you don't necessarily have to own or even use in order to sell them with integrity.

But on the other hand, if you own or are using your competitor's product or service when you could just as easily be using yours, shame on you. Do you really expect to sell anyone when the feeling you're transferring about your product or service isn't even strong enough to motivate *you* to buy it?

Can you see how you could short-circuit your selling efforts and reduce your effectiveness if your feelings are any less than overwhelming about your product or service?

Believe in what you sell. Get enthusiastic about it by *acting* enthusiastic. Make a conscious effort to increase your positive feelings so you can release more of your selling potential.

Selling IS a transference of a feeling. What are *your* feelings?

Chapter 41

$

Action This Day

Her: "If I were your wife, I'd put poison in your coffee."
Him: "If I were your husband, I'd drink it."

The above exchange was reported to have taken place between Lady Astor and Winston Churchill sometime in the 1920's, however, it was actually a joke published in a 1900 edition of *The Chicago Tribune*.

In 1941 Winston Churchill gave his immortal speech which included the following famous lines:

"Never give in, never give in, never, never, never, never–in nothing, great or small, large or petty–never give in except to convictions of honour and good sense. Never yield to force; never yield to the apparently overwhelming might of the enemy."

The application of these powerful words to the sales profession are obvious–persistence has always been the cornerstone of success in sales. But what of the "overwhelming might" Sir Winston mentions in his speech? Most people assume that he was referring to the awesome military power the Nazis wielded at that time, yet the real enemy he had been fighting for several years prior to the actual start of World War II was the overwhelming bias toward a total lack of action by the leaders of the nation Churchill worked so desperately to save.

It is easy to see now, more than 70 years after the end of WWII, that had the British leaders not hesitated for so long to build up their defenses and prepare for Hitler's inevitable move against them, the war would have ended much sooner and many thousands, perhaps hundreds of thousands of lives would have been spared. During those pre-war days, Churchill was virtually a lone voice in the wilderness, warning of what was to come. Yet England's leaders failed to heed that warning, and the overwhelming force of inaction almost cost England its very existence.

Today there is an organization that remembers and honors this great man who saved a nation. The Churchill Centre provides much information about the man, his thoughts and ideas, and his speeches.

 and a special section

It is interesting to note that one particular section of their website that chronicles Churchill's life is titled simply: *Action This Day*. It is not surprising that the summary of Sir Winston Churchill's earthly existence is focused upon the actions that he took, for it is neither thoughts nor ideas nor speeches, but rather action, that is the machine that drives all human achievement, and Churchill was certainly a man of action.

Likewise, within the sales profession, it is action that ultimately produces successful sales results. The overwhelming force of procrastination and inaction must be conquered each day to achieve the desired effect.

It would be beneficial to your career if each and every day you were to ask yourself, "What will be my Action This Day?"

Visit: www.winstonchurchill.org

Chapter 42

$

What's Your Pleasure?

The new pastor's wife had invited some of the prominent ladies from her new church over for dinner. Wanting to make an especially good first impression, she went all out, working long into the night and all the next day to prepare for that evening's gathering.

As she was always receiving compliments from people at her previous parish on how well mannered her young daughters are, she decided to include them in the meeting to further impress her new future lady friends.

Sitting at the table that evening, she suddenly had an idea. Turning to her six-year-old daughter, she said, "Would you like to say the blessing this evening sweetheart?"

"I wouldn't know what to say, mommy," the girl replied.

"Just say what you hear Mommy say," she instructed.

The daughter bowed her head and stated, "Lord, why on earth did I invite so many people to dinner?"

They say that everyone is moving in one of two directions, and knowing in which direction they're heading and what motivates them to do so can unlock the secret to successfully selling to them.

Let's briefly examine these two motivating factors and see how they might help *you* sell more.

On the one hand, there are people who are moving away from pain.

How we define pain depends upon the individual with whom you are dealing.

For example, losing money, *any* amount of money, may be for some the epitome of pain. Just the thought of losing money may cause some people more mental anguish than they're willing to face. These people will buy your product or service if you can show them how much *not* buying will cost them, or, as the late, great Bend Feldman was fond of saying, "If you can show them that it will cost them more *not* to buy, than *to* buy, they *will buy*."

Even if they think your price is higher than your competitor's price, you can point out to them that "It's better to have paid a little more than you need, than to have paid a little less than you should, isn't it?"

Of course, they understand the cost of paying less than they should, because you would first identify, through the proper use of questions, an incident where they lost a lot of money by purchasing something that was inadequate, thus costing them more money than they might have saved from the lower price. This, by the way, is the difference between *price* and *cost*.

The above is only one example of moving away from pain. There are many other types of pain, and for those who are motivated by preventing or relieving pain, *selling the problem* is the correct strategy, because if you can sell them on the problem, they will demand the solution.

On the other hand, we have those people who are moving *toward pleasure*. Again, we define pleasure in accordance with *their* experience, not ours. I find that these people are actually easier to sell, because they know what they want. For these people (and by the way, there are far fewer of them than there are fear-motivated types) you would use the old axiom of, "Sell the sizzle, not the steak." These are the people to whom you sell the *benefits* of your product or service. It is the pleasure of enjoying the benefits that will move these people to action.

But as with our pain example, we must use questions to properly uncover our prospect's idea of pleasure. Perhaps it's not actually enjoying the steak that gives him pleasure, but the feeling he gets from watching his next-door neighbor salivate as that neighbor peeks over the hedge and watches your prospect cooking that steak on his backyard barbecue.

So before you attempt to use either *pain* or *pleasure* motivation, first make sure that you understand what their idea of pain or pleasure is.

Knowing and applying these principles will definitely aid you in your selling, and is guaranteed to bring you more and greater success.

134

Chapter 43

$

The Importance of Asking

I'm always pointing out the importance of asking questions, but it's a good idea to encourage others to ask questions also. For example:

An old blacksmith realized that he was soon going to quit working so hard, so he picked out a strong young man to become his apprentice. The old fellow was crabby and exacting. "Don't ask me a lot of questions," he told the boy, "just do whatever I tell you to do."

One day the old blacksmith took an iron out of the forge and laid it on the anvil. "Get the hammer over there," he said, "and when I nod my head, hit it real good and hard." So the young man did exactly as he was told.

Now the town is looking for a new blacksmith.

Our universe operates by a set of laws and principles. Learning how to use just one of them to your advantage can make more difference in your selling career then a year of cold calling.

Many of these principles are not understood, even by our most brilliant scientists. Gravity is one example. We all know it exists, yet exactly how it works, or what it is for that matter, is still a mystery. But there's no denying that gravity is real. It's a universal law that we have to deal with every day, whether we understand it or not, whether we *believe* in it or not. It dictates our results relative to our actions.

There are many other universal laws and success principles that determine our outcomes relative to how we apply them. To most people, what these success principles are, and how to use them to their advantage, is still a secret. But it shouldn't be. Many of these success principles, and the method for utilizing them, can be found in the most common book in print. Of course I'm referring to the *Holy Bible*. I believe there are a lot of good ideas in the Bible that apply to selling.

I know one verse in particular that says "Seek, and ye shall find." That's not a bad technique for *prospecting*, is it?

Another verse says "Knock, and it shall be opened unto you." That sounds like a good way to start a sales call, don't you think?

There's another verse that says, "Ask, and it shall be given." That's a pretty good closing technique, wouldn't you agree?

These three statements found in the Bible, taken together, make up a very powerful selling system. In his book, *The Magic of Thinking Big*, Dr. David Schwartz highly endorses this formula as a way of getting virtually anything you want. An easy way to remember this formula is to use the three letters of the word ask: A.S.K. A for ask, S for seek, and K for knock.

- Ask and it shall be given
- Seek and you shall find
- Knock and it shall be opened

This simple formula: Ask, Seek, and Knock, represents three separate and distinct components for achieving success. Since it comes from the Bible, the first part, ask, obviously refers to asking God to provide, so begin by getting God involved in your goal.

By the way, if you don't believe in God, or in the Bible, consider this: as a student of success principals for over two decades, I can only say that I've heard too many super achievers attribute their success to what I call the "faith factor" to try to overlook this component or cover it up. After all, who am I to water down the message that was so important to my own success?

So ask means to involve God, which is probably the easiest of the three steps in this formula.

Seek, I believe, means to reach out beyond yourself, to the world around you. You're gathering information and intelligence. You're looking, reading, listening, learning. Applying this to selling would include studying marketing data, brushing up on product knowledge, and reading books that can help you upgrade your knowledge.

Knocking, on the other hand, is a physical action. It's getting the attention of other people. It's sharing your ideas with people, and involving others in your goal. In the case of selling, it would be prospecting, networking, presenting, closing and any other physical task required to make a sale.

So, here we have a success formula that *will* change your sales results forever if you implement it. Ask, seek, and knock.

Most salespeople naturally apply the last two of these components, and do achieve some success. But like opening a safe, where you must have all the numbers of the combination to get to the riches inside, you *must* likewise apply all three of these components to receive the maximum benefit for your efforts.

Do not discount the first component of this formula, for it is the asking that *attracts* success to you. It's much easier, and you can be infinitely more productive, if success is coming to you, rather than you having to go to it. If you "go with the flow," and harmonize with universal laws as they're understood, success always comes easier and faster. That's just the way it works.

Chapter 44

$

A Fantastic
Self Development Resource

As a salesman was unwinding at his favorite watering hole in Los Angeles after a hard day on the road, he happened to listen in on a conversation between two people sitting next to him.

One of the men, a stranger who said his name was Joe, kept referring to famous people by their first name, as though he was close friends with them. This went on for some time, until the salesman could no longer keep quiet.

"Excuse me," the salesman piped up, "but you've mentioned more than two dozen famous and important people, all of whom you claim to know personally. I find that rather hard to believe."

"No, it's true. I hobnob with *all* the rich and famous people. I know them and they know me." Joe said.

Giving this unimpressive stranger the once-over, the salesman stated, "Well, that seems unlikely."

"Okay," Joe replied, "I'll prove it. Go ahead and pick any three famous people, and I'll bet you a hundred dollars that I know them all."

Accepting Joe's challenge, the salesman exclaimed, "You're on! And I know just who I'll pick, too. George Lucas, Bill Gates and the President of the United States."

Immediately, Joe and the salesman left the bar and headed over to the Bonaventure Hotel where George Lucas was appearing at a Star Wars convention. As the two walked up to him, Mr. Lucas shouted out, "Joe! It has been a long time! When are you coming back out to Skywalker Ranch for a visit?"

Surprised, but not totally impressed, the salesman stated to Joe, "Well, this is LA, you probably work in the movie industry."

So the two headed up to Washington State where they called on Bill Gates at his fifty thousand square foot home outside of Seattle. The security guard at the gate waived them right in where Mr. Gates and his guest, Warren Buffett were having lunch. Both he and Mr. Buffett greeted Joe enthusiastically and it was obvious that the three were long time friends.

Still unimpressed, the salesman told Joe, "Well, you might have known Bill Gates before he dropped out of college. You still don't win the bet unless you know the President of the United States."

So the two were off again, this time to New York City where the President was hosting a gathering of most of the world's heads of state at the United Nations. Entering the reception area they could see the President, but security was exceptionally tight and they wouldn't let the salesman get close, so Joe told him to stay put while he went to get the President and bring him over.

Returning alone, Joe apologized to the salesman. "I'm sorry, but the President told me that he's just too busy to come down right now."

Looking dumbfounded, the salesman handed Joe a hundred dollar bill and told him, "That's okay, you win. Here's your hundred dollars."

"I don't understand," Joe said, quite surprised. "You were totally unmoved when you saw that I'm good friends with George Lucas, Bill Gates and Warren Buffett, but *now* you're impressed? What gives?"

The salesman then explained, "While you were up there talking to the President, I overheard the Pope ask the Secretary General of the United Nations, 'who's that guy up there talking to Joe?'"

"I have gathered a posie of other men's flowers, and nothing but the thread that binds them is mine own."

The above words were penned by John Bartlett, a 19th century scholar who became famous for encapsulating the wisdom of many great and successful men, and then publishing their thoughts in the form of a book of quotations that he simply titled *Bartlett's Familiar Quotations*.

One of the many beneficiaries of Bartlett's work was an Englishman who made use of this book nearly half a century after its first printing. In fact, this chap found *Bartlett's Familiar Quotations* to be so essential to his personal development that years later he recommended it in his own book to anyone wishing to better educate themselves.

The book in which he so enthusiastically endorsed *Bartlett's Familiar Quotations* was entitled, *My Early Life*, and the Englishman who authored it was a man who himself became widely quoted among the ranks of the rich and powerful across the globe. I'm referring, of course, to the world famous warrior, politician and statesman, the late Sir Winston Churchill.

Churchill didn't simply read *Bartlett's Familiar Quotations*, he stated that he "studied it intently."

It's reasonable to conclude, then, that a daily infusion of wisdom from people who've successfully accomplished what you're striving to achieve can have a positive impact on your long term results.

With that in mind, I recommend that you add a daily quote to your routine. It is well worth the minute or two that it takes to read a quote from a successful person, especially from a successful salesperson if selling is your profession.

Take Sir Winston's Churchill's advice. I have a feeling that he knew exactly what he was talking about.

142

Chapter 45

$

Selling Through the Language Barrier

In the world of selling, words are the tools of the trade. Many salespeople are often masters of their words, but selling to other cultures where English is not the primary language can add a new dimension to the sales process.

They say that selling is a transference of a feeling from one person to another. See how the words used to convey the messages below make you feel about the products and services they're selling:

- The Dairy Association decided to sell milk in Mexico by using the same approach used in the United States. Soon, "Got Milk?" appeared all across the Nation. The problem? The Spanish translation read "Are you lactating?"

- Not to be out done, Coors took a turn selling to the Hispanic market by promoting their beer with the slogan, "Turn It Loose," which, to the Spanish speaking beer consumers, means "Suffer From Diarrhea."

- Clairol tried selling a curling iron to German consumers. They cleverly coined the phrase "Mist Stick," to describe it. Unfortunately, in German, "mist" is slang for manure.

- Ever sensitive to the impact words have on the sales process, the baby food giant Gerber was very careful with their sales approach when they started selling their product in Africa. No reports of problems with the wording they used, but they did overlook one important non-verbal issue. The jars used the same smiling baby on the label. Later they learned that in

Africa, companies routinely put pictures on the labels of what's inside, since many people can't read.

- When Colgate decided to sell their toothpaste in France, they gave it a very short, simple, easy to remember name: Cue. In France, Cue is also the name of a notorious pornographic magazine.

- Pepsi is an international product, with sales all across the globe. Pitching their wares to over a billion Chinese, Pepsi used their American phrase "Come Alive with the Pepsi Generation." Unfortunately, when translated, the surprised Chinese found that the Americans were proudly boasting that their product "Brings Your Ancestors Back From the Grave!"

- Coca-Cola was not without its challenges in selling to the Chinese market, only this time it was not their claim, but their name. It turned out that in Chinese, the name Coca-Cola means "Bite the wax tadpole" or "female horse stuffed with wax," depending on the dialect. Coke then researched 40,000 characters to find a phonetic equivalent, translating into "happiness in the mouth."

- Frank Perdue has been selling chicken with the slogan, "It takes a strong man to make a tender chicken." When they translated this sales pitch into Spanish, it literally means "it takes an aroused man to make a chicken affectionate."

- Parker Pen sold one of their ball point pens in Mexico with the Spanish version of the phrase "It won't leak in your pocket and embarrass you." Ooops! To millions of Mexicans, Parker proudly proclaimed, "It won't leak in your pocket and make you pregnant!"

- A US based airline ran an advertisement in the Mexican market by pushing first-class comfort with the phrase "Fly in Leather" which, in Spanish, translated to the phrase "Fly Naked."

Chapter 46

$

Selling in a Facebook World

A shepherd was herding his flock of sheep across a country road as a brand new BMW convertible advanced out of a dust cloud toward him. The driver, a young man in an Armani suit, Gucci shoes, Ray Ban sunglasses and Christian Dior tie, stopped just short of the flock and waited anxiously for the sheep to cross. As the shepherd walked in front of his vehicle the driver took a sip of his Starbucks Dulce de Leche latte and suddenly yelled over to him and asked the shepherd, "If I can tell you exactly how many sheep you have in your flock, will you give me one?"

The shepherd looked at the man, obviously a yuppie, then looked at his peacefully grazing flock and calmly answered, "Sure."

The yuppie whipped out his Mack Book Pro laptop computer and logged onto the internet through his wireless connection, where he surfed to the NASA web site and called up a GPS satellite navigation system. Scanning the area, he then opened up an Excel spreadsheet with complex formulas, sent an email on his Blackberry and, after a few minutes, received a response. Finally, he printed out a 150 page report on his mini printer and, turning to the shepherd, stated with total confidence, "You have exactly 1,586 sheep."

"That's correct. You may take one of the sheep" said the shepherd.

He watched the young man select one of the animals and place it in the back seat of his car.

Then the shepherd said to the yuppie: "If I can tell you exactly what your business is, will you give me back the animal?"

"OK, why not" answered the young man.

"Clearly, you are a consultant" said the shepherd.

"That's correct!" said the yuppie, "But how did you guess that?"

"No guessing required" answered the shepherd. "You showed up here without an invitation or request. You expected to be paid for giving me an answer I already knew, to a question I never asked, and you don't know the first thing about my business. Now please give me back my dog."

What do you believe has been the most dramatic change in the world of selling since the year 2000?

I believe that the most significant change is evidenced by the successful companies that have made long term investments in their selling approaches in general and their sales people in particular. By investing time and money in providing state-of-the-art selling tools and then training their salespeople to properly use them, successful sales organizations have been able to seamlessly transition from traditional selling operations of the 20th century to cutting edge 21st century sales leaders.

This is especially true for providing service after the sale. The most successful sales organizations have integrated follow-up and customer service systems into the sales model, making these functions a continuing part of the sales process rather than a separate function run by a different department. This is resulting in higher customer retention, greater repeat business, and more and better quality referrals for those companies that have stayed one step ahead of the game.

In today's highly competitive war for customers, attracting buyers is only one step, but it is the first step. The prospect pool has matured in a virtually socialized Facebook kind of world. More sophisticated buyers today require that successful sales organizations develop different business models and play by different rules. If these customers cannot be satisfied by traditional businesses using 20th century sales approaches, they simply won't buy from them. One consumer recently stated, "If I don't fit into Sprint or Ford or AOL's sales approach, that's not my problem, it's their problem."

How can knowing this help you? Take a look at your calendar and see if you're spending at least twenty five percent of your time on follow up and service functions. I'm not talking about responding to requests or complaints by your customers, I'm referring to proactive tasks that you initiate to keep the customer in the loop after the sale.

Next, make a list of all of the new ideas that you've implemented into your sales approach lately, say, during the past 2 years. Do at least half of these ideas apply to current customers? In other words, are you working as hard to develop methods to serve people who've already bought from you as you are at finding new ways to acquire new business?

Implementing ideas such as regular email contacts in the form of newsletters and the like, or providing free web based tools that your customers can use to make their jobs and their lives easier are two examples of keeping in touch after the sale. And while the new technology of late has made it possible to keep in touch faster, easier and cheaper, don't overlook the opportunity to use these high tech methods to organize such low tech ideas as putting together a pot-luck dinner or other socializing opportunities for your clients.

And one more point for the company presidents and CEOs who are reading this: When the leader's corporate agenda prioritizes sales training and sales follow-up activities, all members of the organization become more focused on the importance of the sales process, which results in a synergy that provides even more and easier sales in the future.

Chapter 47

$

Be Prepared

Girl: "Daddy, can I have ten dollars?"
Father: "No."
Girl: "Then can I have five dollars?"
Father: "No."
Girl: "How about three dollars?"
Father: "No."
Girl: "Two dollars?"
Father: "No."
Girl: "Daddy, can I have one dollar?"
Father: "No."
Girl: "When I grow up, I'm going to be a sales person."
Father: "Why on earth would you want to be a sales person?"
Girl: "Because I'm so used to being told 'no' all the time, I might as well get paid for it!"

When my daughter, Alexandra, was seven years old, she belonged to a group called the American Heritage Girls. It's a church based group similar to the Girl Scouts. Her troop was selling candles to raise money to pay expenses, and as I was working at my desk, Alexandra came into my office, held up the product brochure and immediately began to give me her pitch. It is reproduced here word for word exactly as she told it to me. I don't have a photographic memory, but I do have a voice recorder that I keep on my desk, and I used it to record her presentation. It went like this:

"Hello, my name is Alexandra, and I'm welcoming you to buy any of these you want. For a specialty, there's a lid and candle holder. And also for one of the best candles, there's the Blessings Collection. And you can also get some cookie mix for only eight dollars apiece. So, are you interested in any of this?"

She composed this little pitch the night before, completely on her own. Then she repeated it over and over to herself until she had it memorized. Then she sprang it on me the next day.

She had no help or encouragement from anyone. No one told her to write a script, she just knew from living with a professional salesman that you need to have a presentation if you want to sell something successfully.

After she tried her pitch out on me, I complimented her on what a great job she had done, and told her that I would refine it for her so she could go out and sell her candles.

I tweaked her script a bit, then gave it back to her and told her that after she had it memorized, I would take her door to door.

In addition to revising her script, I also designed a one page order form to be filled out by the prospect. There was a tear off receipt at the bottom. These were placed on a clipboard which had a calculator attached to it so the prospect could calculate the totals for the order. Alexandra would ask the prospect what they liked the best, and when they showed an interest, she would hand them the clipboard, taking the brochure from them and holding it open so they could continue to see the products while they filled out the order form. At the top of the form was a short explanation of who the American Heritage Girls are and why Alexandra was selling the products.

This system allowed her to successfully sell the products on her own (I listened in from around a corner or behind the bushes).

Surprisingly, I learned that Alexandra was the only girl who actually went out and sold the candles this way. This is because her troop was not advised to actually sell the candles. Instead, the mothers were encouraged to sell them to their friends and relatives.

150

Obviously I had a different opinion. Alexandra was in this program to learn valuable skills, and selling candles seemed like a great way to acquire several of them, not the least of which are self confidence and self reliance. This is why, even though I am a sales professional, I didn't sell any candles for her.

After the sale was over, I shared Alexandra's success with the troop leader, suggesting that for the next fund raiser, I might make myself available to train the girls to do as Alexandra had done.

She was not impressed. She even tried to sell me on the idea that it would not work, pointing out that the troop could not afford to buy clipboards for all the girls.

Of course, the cost of clipboards would have been covered by whatever products were sold in the first fifteen minutes of selling, but I didn't bother to share that fact with her, as I don't waste my time with negative thinkers. As a professional sales consultant, I charge a lot of money to advise and train sales organizations, and if she didn't want to receive my services for free, I certainly wasn't going to try to talk her into it.

Even though this group needed additional funds, the girls were not encouraged to sell the products because they were not prepared to do the job successfully.

But given the proper tools (script, clipboard w/calculator and the order forms) and the proper training, Alexandra was able to successfully sell her product much quicker and easier than the other girls–or their parents for that matter.

On a final note, as we were preparing the order forms, Alexandra asked me why I put so much work into the preparation, such as scoring the dashed lines on each paper that separated the order form above from the customer receipt below so that they would separate easily when needed. She was surprised at how much attention to detail I put into these little things. She was really impressed by this.

I explained to her that preparation is necessary to allow the sale to go smoothly. This makes it easy for the prospect to buy, and most success is in direct proportion to the amount of preparation that is made prior to the actual event.

It's ironic that when I was in the boy scouts our motto was *Be Prepared.* Now, almost 40 years later, my daughter was learning this lesson for herself in a similar organization.

As Arthur Ashe had stated, "One important key to success is self confidence. An important key to self confidence is preparation."

Chapter 48

$

Smile!

One bright fourth of July afternoon, a man and a little boy entered a barbershop together. After the man had received a shave, a shampoo, a haircut, and a manicure, he placed the boy in the chair.

"I'm going to buy a new tie to wear for the parade," he said. "I'll be back in a few minutes."

When the barber finished with the boy's haircut, he noticed that the man still hadn't returned. "Looks like your daddy has forgotten all about you," the barber joked.

"That man wasn't my daddy," the boy replied, "he just walked up to me on the street and told me that we were both going to get a free haircut!"

Not too long ago, my wife said something to me that really got my attention. She asked me, "Paul, how do you feel today?"

I answered, "I feel great, why do you ask?"

And she replied, "Maybe you should notify your face."

Good point. You know, the Chinese have a phrase that says, "He who cannot smile should not keep shop."

When I first began selling, I observed people who were well liked, and I noticed that they always smiled. You probably know people like this. Even when they're not particularly happy about something, they have a smile on their face.

I made smiling my number one rule for presenting myself. I smiled all the time, everywhere I went. At first, it felt fake (because it was), and I had to keep remembering to do it. But eventually, over time, it

153

became second nature to me, and I found that I was smiling a lot more.

But more importantly, I began to attract more people to me, and get a better reception from people I approached. The results were well worth the effort.

If you want to sell more, make your prospects–and everybody else for that matter–feel welcome. Smile, even if you don't feel like it!

Every now and then I'll hear someone say "I don't believe in being phony and smiling all the time." But I believe that even a forced smile is better for business than a sincere frown.

What do you think?

Chapter 49

$

The Process of Innovation

Ideas that never got off the ground:

- A waterproof towel
- A book on how to read
- Powdered water
- An inflatable dart board
- Waterproof tea bags
- An ejector seat for helicopters

> *"He that will not apply new remedies must expect new evils: for time is the greatest innovator."*
> Francis Bacon

History teaches us that cotton was grown in India, China, Egypt and Pakistan thousands of years ago, but farming cotton was expensive and labor intensive, requiring hundreds of man hours to separate the cottonseed from the raw cotton fibers. Eli Whitney's idea for the cotton gin in 1794 lead to an innovation in the seed separation process, marking the beginnings of the profitable cotton industry.

Alexander Graham Bell's invention of the telephone resulted from an idea he had for improving the telegraph, and that idea eventually led to the innovation that changed the world and brought about the multi-billion dollar communications industry.

The light bulb, as every school child knows, was invented by Thomas Edison. A man of many ideas, Edison held 1,093 US patents in his name, but it is the light bulb for which Edison is best remembered. In fact,

155

the image of a light bulb above someone's head is often used as the symbol to represent the moment when that person has an idea.

A brilliant idea may, and often does, come to someone in a flash, easily and without effort. We call this inspiration. But innovation is not simply inspiration, it's the combination of inspiration, passion and persistence.

Once you experience inspiration in the form of a brilliant idea, you then face two major barriers to innovation: perfecting the idea, and then selling it. Innovation is a process by which old ways of doing things are pushed aside in favor of a better way.

History is filled with examples of people who were inspired with great ideas but were not innovators. Before the Wright Brother's flight in 1903, hundreds of people attempted to fly in gliders, airships, balloons and other fantastic contraptions. They were often regarded as daredevils, kooks, and eccentrics, but they did not raise our lifestyles to a higher level. They had ideas, they may have even been inventers, but they were not innovators.

Innovative people are passionate about something, and will labor long and hard to make their ideas work. They'll risk financial loss, ridicule, and bodily injury. In short, innovators will risk pretty much everything to turn their inspiration into reality. And when they finally have their prototype working, they'll risk everything all over again to sell others on using their new invention.

You'd think that this would be the easy part. "Build a better mousetrap," goes the saying, "and the world will beat a path to your door." But the fact is, until a new idea is successfully sold, it can't change the world.

Often, the people who put up the most resistance are the people who could benefit the most, those who could sell or implement the invention in their own business.

Tailors, concerned for their livelihood, smashed the first sewing machines.

Ken Olson, President of Digital Equipment Corporation, is known for making the now infamous statement that, "There is no need for any individual to have a computer in their home."

And although the cause and cure for scurvy was discovered in England in the early 1600's, it wasn't until the mid 1700's that this knowledge was accepted by the English authorities and the cure implemented.

But innovators keep on plugging away. They keep selling and they don't give up until momentum builds to a point where the idea finally becomes an everyday part of the average person's life, so commonplace as to almost be an afterthought, and society has risen to a new level.

Inspiration, passion and persistence. This is the process of innovation.

158

Chapter 50

$

How to Achieve an
Unfair Competitive Advantage

> *"If you don't have a competitive advantage, don't compete."*
>
> Jack Welch

A small town's first strip mall had finished construction and the new store owners were busy making their final preparations for the grand opening celebration. As the big day neared, however, it soon became apparent that there was a problem for three of the proprietors. All three of them were opening stores that specialized in the sale of video electronics–TVs, plasma screens, VCRs, DVD players, and home theaters. To make matters worse, all three stores were side-by-side.

Each owner noticed the problem, but none said anything to the others.

With only two days until the grand opening, a huge sign arrived and was installed above the shop on the left which read: *Best Deals In Town.*

The next day, another huge sign was delivered and installed above the shop on the right that declared: *Lowest Prices In The County.*

Finally, very early on the morning of opening day, a small neon sign was hung above the door of the middle shop which read: *Main Entrance.*

When Coca-Cola first came on the market, it was sold at soda fountains in drug stores and in coffee shops. You've probably never heard this little story, but early on, a guy had an idea that he offered to Coke. He wrote to the president an intriguing letter offering to help them double the business. He said something like, "For one million dollars, I will tell you how to double the business of Coca Cola with two words."

The president of Coke called him down to Atlanta, sized up the guy as competent and serious, and said, "Okay."

The guy's two words: "Bottle it!"

Today, Coke is a giant in the soft drink market and the Coca-Cola brand is reportedly recognized by ninety four percent of the world's population.

When scanning the business world, it's not uncommon for even a casual observer to note that giants dominate the landscape. Unless your company happens to be one of them, you have a major uphill battle in gaining share in virtually any segment of the market today.

This is true whether you're the owner of a small company, the president or CEO of a medium sized firm, or even an individual sales rep. Everything is relative, and for the vast majority of people slugging it out for their piece of the American consumer's pocketbook, there's always a competitor that is bigger and more entrenched with which to contend.

Most people entering this arena make the mistake of going up against these giants, confident that their better idea or superior product or lower price will give them the victory. They see themselves as David who defeated the much bigger and stronger Goliath.

But what they fail to understand, and what the failure rate of new business ventures and the churn rate of new sales reps has demonstrated time and again, is that the tale of David vs. Goliath is novel for the simple reason that things were never what they appeared to be.

They overlook the fact that David was not just a small boy who tended sheep, he was a young adult, a professional marksman, an expert with one of the most deadly weapons of his time.

You see, as a shepherd, part of David's job description was to protect the sheep from predators, and David had a history of success in this area. He had killed a bear and he had killed a lion, two predators much faster, tougher and stronger than any oversized man with a bad attitude. David had the confidence of knowing exactly what he was capable of, and he also had the advantage of being underestimated.

So when you analyze the situation, taking into account all of the factors, it was really Goliath who was the underdog in this scenario.

In the business world, however, these giants are exactly what they appear to be: bigger, richer, and more established. To presume to be able to beat them at their own game would be–and has been for countless individuals and corporations–a fatal mistake, at least from a financial standpoint.

So how can you compete? This is where the unfair competitive advantage comes into play.

Anthony E. Whyte is President of the American Institute of Management Technology. For over 30 years as President and CEO, Tony has founded and directed operations of a number of business information service companies such as AMR International, ListenUSA!, The American Payroll Institute, Media Network International, and others. He has fostered deceptively simple collaborative partnerships with organizations across the United States and around the globe.

Tony is a brilliant businessman and a terrific guy, and he is a master of achieving and exploiting an unfair competitive advantage. Rather than attacking the market leaders, Tony has successfully leveraged the power of these giants for his own benefit many times during his career, and you can learn to do the same.

You see, Tony understands the old schoolyard rule that says you can avoid a lot of beatings from the mean kids by making friends with the toughest one of them. It doesn't even have to be one of the kids in your class.

Tony advocates finding a way to appeal to one of the market leaders in a non-competitive fashion so as to secure their involvement in a mutually beneficial partnership. In this way, you've not only removed the risk of having Goliath come after you, but you've also secured a level of protection from some of the other giants as well.

For example, some years ago Tony was setting up a series of eight information technology conferences for CEOs in major cities across the United States. Tony was going up against a lot of contenders for this market, not the least of which were the major universities. As one of the largest IT training organizations in the world, IBM would also be considered a *major* competitor in this field, but rather than going up *against* these giants, Tony decided to win some of the giants over to his side. In fact, he was in the process of securing a partnership agreement with four of them. Here's what happened next:

Tony was planning on having a major computer hardware company, a major software company, a major communications company, and a major management consulting firm participate. The following is an excerpt from a conversation Tony had with a marketing representative of IBM. Let's listen in...

Tony: "Michelle, have you had a chance to review our prospectus about the CEO Road-Show Events?"

Michelle: "Yes, as a matter of fact I have, there's just one problem."

Tony: "What's that?"

Michelle: "Well, we don't want to be one of four sponsors, we want to be THE sponsor!"

Tony: "Hey, no problem, we'd be honored to work with IBM exclusively, how would you like to get started?"

Michelle: "Whoa! Slow down, we need to look at this a couple of ways."

Tony: "Okay, well, what do you need?"

Michelle: "Well, we're not quite sure whether we want to do one big splashy event, say in Washington DC, or whether we want to do the eight Road Shows. Can you send me the costs of each?

Tony: "Sure, you'll have the info in a few days. Probably by mid next week, okay?"

Michelle: "Fine, rush it to me. Thanks, talk to you then."

Needless to say, Tony worked all weekend to get the package together. Fast forward to the following Thursday...

Tony: "Michelle, have you had the chance to review the info?"

Michelle: "Yes, and we've decided what we want to do, too."

Tony: "Yes, what's that?

Michelle: "We want to do both, but we have to start with the Big Event in Washington DC on May 8. We've got Lou Gerstner (the Chairman of IBM at the time) on the schedule to appear on the program in the morning. It's Small Business Week, and the town will be filled with CEOs of all shapes and sizes," She went on, "and we want you to coordinate the other seven events in the other major cities with each of the seven IBM Regional Managers, and these are very active guys and ladies who have pretty jammed schedules already."

Tony: "It will be done!"

IBM assisted Tony by providing to him over four million dollars for his project, as well as contributing the time and energy of their many people who were involved. I would say that this kind of contribution constitutes an unfair competitive advantage.

Looking back at our David vs. Goliath example, we can see that Tony Whyte didn't invent the idea of finding a bigger kid on the block with which to partner. If you read the text carefully, you will see that Goliath was NOT the biggest combatant in this famous battle. David's words make it clear that he had already secured an unfair competitive advantage before the battle was ever fought:

Speaking directly to Goliath, David said, "This day will the Lord deliver thee into mine hand...the battle is the Lord's, and HE will give you into our hands."

Follow Tony's lead and take a lesson from a young shepherd who became king: Identify how what you do can incidentally serve the biggest player in the game, strike a deal, and secure for yourself an unfair competitive advantage.

SUCCESS!

About the Author

Paul David French discovered the principles of No Objection Selling as a result of an intensive self development program he undertook to overcome his extremely analytical approach and introverted style. He quickly become the top producer of the largest property and casualty insurance company in the State of Michigan during his rookie year in spite of his lack of sales experience, knowledge, skills or contacts. Paul's implementation of No Objection Selling also allowed him to achieve his company's highest client retention and lowest loss ratio simultaneously, giving him the most profitable book of business per premium dollar in the company.

Since then, Paul has consulted with many business owners and top executives across the U.S. and is the founder and president of NOS Marketing, a marketing and consulting firm that specializes in developing unique sales approaches and providing sales training based upon the principles of No Objection Selling.

You can contact Paul by sending an email to: pfrench@noobjectionselling.com

Or visit: www.noobjectionselling.com

Also by Paul David French:
The Awesome Power of No Objection Selling

How to take 'no' for an answer and make more sales than you ever dreamed possible.

Most books on selling attempt to instruct salespeople how to "overcome" sales objections. What they really want is a book that shows them how to easily eliminate all of the unnecessary effort and instead sell more without ever having to even deal with objections. This book does exactly that. Nowhere else will you find this kind of resource.

"The No Objection Selling concepts are highly unique, new, not available elsewhere, and totally effective."
- Anthony E. Whyte
President, American Institute of Management Technology

"Rather than requiring a salesperson to memorize and master a multitude of responses to sales objections, Paul's book simply and elegantly eliminates them entirely from the sales process."
- Matthew E. May
Author of *In Pursuit of Elegance*

"I loved reading The Awesome Power of No Objection Selling because Paul tells it like it is and then instructs, step-by-step, how to sell big, sell well, and develop a returning and referring clientele."
- Elinor Stutz
Author of *Nice Girls DO Get the Sale:
Relationship Building That Gets Results*

"After reading this book you will know more about 'why people buy' and how to easily and successfully sell to them than 99% of all professional salespeople."
- Eric Wong
Senior Vice President, Capital One Bank

Order at www.noobjectionselling.com